ON LOVE

ON LOVE

A Philosophical Dialogue

Nicholas J. Pappas

Algora Publishing
New York

Library of Congress Cataloging-in-Publication Data —

Names: Pappas, Nicholas J., author.
Title: Love / Nicholas J. Pappas.
Description: New York : Algora Pub., 2016.
Identifiers: LCCN 2016001483| ISBN 9781628941890 (soft cover : alk. paper) |
    ISBN 9781628941906 (hard cover : alk. paper) | ISBN 9781628941913 (eBook)
Subjects: LCSH: Love. | Interpersonal attraction. | Friendship. |
    Interpersonal relations.
Classification: LCC BD436 .P35 2016 | DDC 128/.46--dc23 LC record available at
http://lccn.loc.gov/2016001483

Printed in the United States

Nuptial love maketh mankind; friendly love perfecteth it; but wanton love corrupteth and embaseth it.

— Francis Bacon, "Of Love" (1612)

TABLE OF CONTENTS

Introduction

This book consists of one long conversation between Director and Handsome on the topic of love.

Who are these characters? Why don't they have traditional names?

Director is the one constant throughout the books I've written. He is a philosopher, and he does what you might expect a philosopher to do. Handsome appears only in this book. He is, as you might guess, handsome.

From Director's name we gather that he, well, directs. When I first conceived of him, I saw him as working in a company as a manager. That happened to be at a time when I, too, was working in a company as a manager. But, and I can't stress this enough — Director isn't, and never was, me. None of my characters are me. None of my characters are anyone else in real life, for that matter.

Director is my idea of a philosopher. As such, he helps lead the conversations in my books. His name reminds us that he is often directing, even when he does so in less than obvious ways.

And isn't this how it once was? Someone named Weaver wove. Someone named Baker baked. So it is with my characters.

But what does Handsome do? He simply is; he is handsome. Naming him Handsome allowed me to keep present to the reader his looks throughout the conversation, as happens in life. But after a while, ideally, the name becomes merely a name. One forgets, or rather discounts the fact, that the other is good looking (or bad looking, or passing indifferent). One focuses simply on what is said.

And what is said is meant to be basic, simple. In my opinion, this is how we get to the fundamental. Accordingly, there is no prerequisite for a good understanding of this book.

I found the above quote from Francis Bacon, though it may seem dated, to be especially appropriate because of what it says about perfecting mankind. My book is about love in general, but I trust you'll sense an underlying concern with what he calls friendly love.

I hope you enjoy it.

— Nick Pappas

1. PLAY

Handsome: I once wrote a one act play on love, you know.

Director: You did? Why am I only learning of this now?

Handsome: Because it wasn't very good.

Director: Well, give me the idea of it and let me decide for myself.

Handsome: Alright. There are three characters, and they're in a bar.

Director: At what time of day?

Handsome: Mid-afternoon.

Director: Was it a week day or weekend day?

Handsome: Week day.

Director: Were these people supposed to be at work?

Handsome: Yes.

Director: An interesting setting for the topic of love. So what happens?

Handsome: The older two tease the younger one for falling in love too easily.

Director: Is the younger the sort that goes around falling in love here and falling in love there — always somehow in love with someone?

Handsome: Yes, exactly.

Director: How does the play resolve?

Handsome: Well, that's it — it doesn't really.

Director: You wrote a play with no resolution?

Handsome: What can I say? I told you it wasn't very good.

Director: And the action is nothing more than the young one being teased?

Handsome: Yes. Bad, don't you think?

Director: Not necessarily. Does the teasing bring out what the young one thinks about love?

Handsome: Yes, it does. He thinks that love is nothing more than a feeling, and that all feelings of love are good.

Director: And what do the older two think?

Handsome: They both think the young one doesn't know what love is. And so as they tease him, they tell him what it is.

Director: What do they say?

Handsome: One of them says love is commitment. The other says love is a lie.

Director: Did you intend one of these three views to be more persuasive than the others?

Handsome: I wanted love as a feeling and love as commitment to blend and form a new view that prevails. But I couldn't quite get it to work out that way.

Director: And that's why there's no resolution to the play?

Handsome: Right. No one view comes out on top.

Director: Why do you think that happened?

Handsome: Because I set out writing in order to clarify my view, to really learn what I think about love — and I failed. Pathetic, isn't it?

Director: Don't be too hard on yourself. After all, you must have learned something from your playwriting experience. Didn't you?

Handsome: Sure I did. I learned that you should know what you think before you write.

Director: If you could clear up your thoughts, if you could come to know love through and through — would you be willing to go back and write another play?

Handsome: I'd be willing to do that.

Director: Good. So let's talk about love.

2. HANDSOME

Handsome: Where will we start?

Director: With the obvious. But that means I'm going to tell you something, and I don't want you to get upset.

Handsome: I promise I won't get upset.

Director: Well, you must have figured out by now — that you're a handsome man.

Handsome: So now you're going to tease me?

Director: Who's teasing? I'm telling you the truth. And the question I have is whether you recognize this truth.

Handsome: People do tell me I'm handsome.

Director: So why am I bringing this up?

Handsome: I'd like to know.

Director: Because it might have an influence on your thinking about love. But let's flip things around. Can you imagine being very ugly?

Handsome: I can.

Director: How would that influence your thinking about love?

Handsome: I'm not sure it would.

Director: Love is love?

Handsome: Of course.

Director: But what would your choices be?

Handsome: What do you mean?

Director: I mean, if you're handsome, don't you think you have one set of choices, and if you're ugly you have another?

Handsome: True enough.

Director: Do you think your choices might affect your thinking?

Handsome Yes, but we all have a different set of choices. So let me tell you what the key is, regardless of the choices you have.

Director: What?

Handsome: Never allow yourself to be attracted to someone who's not attracted to you.

Director: Easier said than done! But what does this mean for the ugly?

Handsome: It means they have to find those that they're attracted to who are attracted to them for something other than their looks.

Director: And what might that 'something other' be?

Handsome: It could be any number of things.

Director: Can you give me an example?

Handsome: Sure. Their brains.

3. ROUGHLY MATCHED

Director: Ah, the brain. What's the brain known for?

Handsome: You're asking me seriously? Intelligence.

Director: Can love be founded on intelligence alone?

Handsome: Well, people can be attracted to intelligence. But love takes more than that.

Director: What more?

Handsome: It takes heart and soul.

Director: You mean good, strong heart and soul — and on both sides of the relationship?

Handsome: Yes. The lovers have to be roughly matched in their goodness and their strength.

Director: Do they need to be roughly matched in anything else?

Handsome: Well, if you want me to be honest....

Director: Of course I do.

Handsome: Physical beauty. You need a rough match in terms of that.

Director: Really? So the beautiful and the not-so-beautiful are doomed to mate with their own?

Handsome: Oh, don't get me wrong. There are plenty of exceptions. But that's the rule.

Director: And is there a rule for intelligence?

Handsome: There is. It's usually best if there's a rough match in that, as well.

Director: And that's all there is to it? Intelligence, heart and soul, and looks?

Handsome: No, there's one more thing.

Director: What?

Handsome: It helps to have a roughly matched pair — of beautiful minds.

4. Beautiful Minds

Director: Beautiful minds? But what do you mean by 'mind'? And what distinguishes it from the brain?

Handsome: Mind is what you do with your brain.

Director: So if you put your brain to good use you come to have a beautiful mind?

Handsome: Exactly.

Director: And is this irrespective of the amount of intelligence involved?

Handsome: Yes. Even those with the least intelligence can have a beautiful mind. Just as those with the greatest intelligence can have an ugly mind.

Director: But tell me. Just how attractive is a beautiful mind?

Handsome: What do you mean?

Director: I'm wondering if you can't be happily in love with nothing but beauty of mind.

Handsome: Well, I don't know about that.

Director: Why not?

Handsome: What if the person has a rotten heart and soul?

Director: You can have a beautiful mind with a rotten heart and soul?

Handsome: Oh, yes. Definitely.

Director: How?

Handsome: Like this. Suppose someone uses their brain to do beautiful work as an inventor, work that benefits a great many people. But then suppose he or she is just rotten through and through when it comes to dealing with others.

Director: I see what you mean. Then let's say the person we're talking about doesn't have a rotten heart and soul.

Handsome: But this person has little intelligence and not-so-good looks?

Director: Yes.

Handsome: I have to admit, Director — for me, loving someone like that would be hard.

Director: But what about the young one in your play?

Handsome: What about him?

Director: Would he fall in love simply with beauty of mind, assuming heart and soul are fine?

Handsome: It's funny you should ask. He thinks he would. But what he really falls in love with is looks.

Director: And the older two know this and so they tease him?

Handsome: Yes. But you know, in an earlier draft I did have him focus on beauty of mind, just not in a way you'd expect.

Director: How so?

Handsome: He was attracted to those who have minds less beautiful than his own.

Director: Why on earth would he be attracted to people like that?

Handsome: I'm embarrassed to say, even on my character's behalf.

Director: Say it, Handsome.

Handsome: The ones with the less beautiful minds make him feel... superior.

5. SUPERIOR

Director: Superior at what?

Handsome: What do you mean?

Director: I mean, what does it mean to feel superior without saying at what?

Handsome: He feels superior because he dictates the terms of his relationships by manipulating the ones he's with.

Director: And that's a good use of his brain?

Handsome: He thinks it is. But you're making me feel ashamed.

Director: Why should you be ashamed? We're talking about a character, not you. And the character we're talking about was just a draft.

Handsome: True.

Director: But I have to admit, Handsome. I'm curious about the mindset of this character. Can you tell me more?

Handsome: Of course. For someone like him it's all about sex, though he would deny it if asked. And –

Director: But hold on. Is it about sex or is it about superiority?

Handsome: Honestly? It's about both.

Director: So he's a very low type of character.

Handsome: Yes, he is.

Director: Then let's just get to the bottom line. How does he define good use of the brain?

Handsome: As getting what you want.

Director: But that's not how your final version of the character sees it, is it?

Handsome: No, of course not.

Director: What's good use for him?

Handsome: Learning to appreciate others.

6. Appreciation, Equality

Director: Hmm. What do you say we set your play aside but take things up from here, from appreciation, and see where they lead? Do you have any objection?

Handsome: No, of course not.

Director: Good. So how do you define appreciation?

Handsome: You know. Appreciation is just... appreciation.

Director: Can we say appreciation is the recognition and enjoyment of worth?

Handsome: Yes, definitely

Director: Then tell me. If someone appreciates you, don't you think it would be best if you could appreciate that person in turn?

Handsome: Naturally, yes.

Director: And isn't that how it should be when it comes to your mate?

Handsome: You mean there should be reciprocal appreciation?

Director: Yes. Don't you agree?

Handsome: I certainly do.

Director: And for that it doesn't matter how much of a certain quality someone has?

Handsome: What do you mean?

Director: I mean, suppose someone is more intelligent than you. Can you appreciate her?

Handsome: If there's still a rough match of intelligence, yes.

Director: And if there isn't?

Handsome: She's much more intelligent than I am? I don't see how I'd be able to form a good appreciation of her.

Director: Why not?

Handsome: How can I truly appreciate something I don't share?

Director: Do you really need to share in something in order to appreciate it? I mean, can't I appreciate a fine athlete without being nearly as athletic?

Handsome: You have a point.

Director: And can't I appreciate a fine artist without being nearly as artistic?

Handsome: You can.

Director: Isn't it the same when it comes to intelligence?

Handsome: That follows from what we're saying.

Director: But why do you seem like you don't want to agree? Is it because you can't feel superior if someone is more intelligent?

Handsome: Of course not. Superiority isn't the point.

Director: What is?

Handsome: Feeling equal to your mate. And if she's more intelligent than I am, or whatever, how am I going to feel equal?

Director: That's simple. You feel equal when you appreciate one another equally, regardless of anything else.

Handsome: You really think that's how it works?

Director: Yes.

7. ROLES

Handsome: Well, I have a hard time believing it.

Director: Why?

Handsome: Look. Why don't we stand up?

Director: Here? In the café?

Handsome: Yes. I want to show you something.

Director: Alright. What do you want to show me?

Handsome: Let's role play.

Director: Okay.

Handsome: Hello, Director. How are you today?

Director: We're playing ourselves?

Handsome: Yes. So just answer my question.

Director: I'm fine thanks, Handsome. How are you?

Handsome: Good. Let's stop and sit back down. What did you learn?

Director: I'm not sure I learned anything.

Handsome: But weren't you paying attention?

Director: To what?

Handsome: To me!

Director: I don't understand.

Handsome: Well, I was paying attention to you. Do you want to know what I saw?

Director: Sure.

Handsome: I saw someone with alert and penetrating eyes.

Director: Penetrating? Really? What do such eyes tell you?

Handsome: They tell you you're dealing with someone who's very intelligent. And now I should tell you about your face.

Director: What about it?

Handsome: It was composed.

Director: What does that tell you?

Handsome: That you're in command of yourself. And now I'll tell you about your body language.

Director: Please do.

Handsome: You were standing upright and firm where you were planted.

Director: And what does that tell you?

Handsome: That you're confident. Now what about me?

Director: What about you?

Handsome: I'm none of those things! So if someone has those qualities, which I admire, how am I possibly going to feel equal to her, regardless of how she appreciates me?

8. Self-Esteem?

Director: I think you have low self-esteem.

Handsome: Ha! I could have told you that.

Director: What do you think it takes to have a healthy amount of self-esteem?

Handsome: It takes love.

Director: Love? Really?

Handsome: I'm just telling you my experience.

Director: Then tell me more.

Handsome: Well, first I should say that I've mostly only known one-sided love.

Director: You mean someone loves you but you don't love her, or you love someone but she doesn't love you?

Handsome: Yes.

Director: And which sort of one-sided love makes for self-esteem?

Handsome: When someone loves me. But there's a problem with that.

Director: I'm sure there is.

Handsome: The love is fleeting.

Director: People start loving you and then they stop?

Handsome: No. I'm the one who puts an end to things.

Director: Why do you do that?

Handsome: Because it's not enough to feel a little boost of self-esteem.

Director: What more do you need?

Handsome: Mutual attraction.

Director: Wouldn't you have that with someone who appreciates you as much as you appreciate her?

Handsome: Appreciation is different than attraction. You can appreciate someone and not be attracted to them.

Director: Just as you can be attracted to someone and not appreciate them?

Handsome: Yes.

Director: Have you had mutual appreciation?

Handsome: To a certain degree.

Director: But there was no mutual attraction?

Handsome: Correct.

Director: Have you had mutual attraction?

Handsome: Equal attraction? I don't know.

Director: What do you mean you don't know?

Handsome: I can never tell these things.

Director: Why not?

Handsome: My lack of self-esteem always gets in the way.

Director: How so?

Handsome: When I'm attracted to someone, and I don't know if she's attracted to me, or how much she's attracted to me — I lose my nerve.

Director: So you never take steps to learn how she feels?

Handsome: Right.

9. ATTRACTION

Director: Tell me. How often are you attracted to someone? Once a year? Once a month? What?

Handsome: Honestly? I'm attracted to someone just about every day.

Director: What? Every day? This is a serious case! And what are you expecting, or at least half expecting — that these women you're attracted to will make the first move and confess their love for you and that will solve the problem?

Handsome: Yes.

Director: Yes? Is it possible? What about the women who are attracted to you but you're not attracted to? How often do they confess their love to you? Every day?

Handsome: More or less.

Director: I'm in shock. How do they do this? Do they all walk right up and say, I love you?

Handsome: Of course not. Their body language says it all.

Director: You mean they plant their feet firmly and show confidence, as we were saying?

Handsome: No, not that.

Director: What then?

Handsome: They get all sweet.

Director: Sweet?

Handsome: Yes, dreamy even.

Director: And let me guess — forgetful, too, if we can say forgetfulness has its own type of body language?

Handsome: Yes, that too.

Director: And that's what's been giving you those little boosts of self-esteem? These declarations of love?

Handsome: Pitiful, isn't it?

Director: But what do you do if one of them actually confesses her love to you in so many words? I assume that happens.

Handsome: It happens. And believe it or not? I'm tempted to confess my love in return.

Director: Now I'm truly amazed. Why?

Handsome: Because in that actual moment I think I do love her, in a way.

Director: You love her? In a way? But why?

Handsome: Because she loves me. But I don't tell her I love her.

Director: Because you're aware that five minutes later someone else will be in love with you and you'll love her in return for her loving you?

Handsome: Right, and so I say nothing and break things off.

10. NOTHING

Director: Yes, this is a very serious case indeed.

Handsome: What can I do?

Director: Fight the nothing.

Handsome: What do you mean?

Director: These five-minute love affairs of yours — what do they amount to, aside from fuel for your ego?

Handsome: I guess they don't amount to anything.

Director: They amount to nothing. Yes?

Handsome: Yes. But what does it mean to fight the nothing?

Director: It means you turn to the ones you're attracted to.

Handsome: And make the first move?

Director: If necessary? Yes.

Handsome: But then what?

Director: You see how they react.

Handsome: And if they react well?

Director: You make another move, and so on.

Handsome: But where does it all lead?

Director: Where do you want it to lead?

Handsome: I'm afraid of where I want it to lead.

Director: What, marriage?

Handsome: Yes.

Director: Why are you afraid of marriage? Is it because you'd have to trade in all your little love affairs for one great big love affair?

Handsome: If that were really how it would work, I'd say great — sign me up. But that might not be how it works.

11. SOMETHING

Director: Do you want to know how it works?

Handsome: Of course I do.

Director: It works when a marriage is founded not on nothing, but on something.

Handsome: But what's 'something'?

Director: There are many kinds of something. But we can reduce them all down to one thing.

Handsome: What?

Director: Are you sure you want to know?

Handsome: Of course!

Director: Common interest.

Handsome: But then you're saying working marriages aren't based on love?

Director: On the kind of love-you-because-you-love-me that you described? No, of course they're not based on that.

Handsome: But there's a love that goes with common interest — isn't there?

Director: If it's true common interest? Yes, a very great love.

Handsome: And is it that the common interest derives from the love, or that the love derives from the common interest?

Director: It's hard to say. And I'm not sure it matters much, anyway. What matters is that there's lasting love. No?

Handsome: Of course. But what are we really talking about? I mean, on the one hand the common interest might be that you simply enjoy spending time with one another. Right?

Director: Right.

Handsome: And on the other hand the common interest might be that you help to advance each other's career. But should you love someone for that?

Director: Solely for that? Of course not.

Handsome: Now you've really got me wondering. What would you say is the embodiment of common interest love?

Director: The embodiment? Aside from the individuals involved?

Handsome: Yes.

Director: Well, the first thing that comes to mind is the home. What do you think?

Handsome: I think that's exactly so.

Director: Is that something you'd like? A home filled with love?

Handsome: Who wouldn't?

Director: But what if there's more than love?

Handsome: What do you mean?

Director: What if there are two people living in that home — who are living up to their potential?

12. BEST

Handsome: That would be all the better!

Director: How do you think that might happen?

Handsome: I suppose two people can inspire one another.

Director: Yes, but how do you know if someone will inspire you to the full?

Handsome: It's probably just something I'd feel.

Director: But if you wanted to go by more than just feel?

Handsome: We'd have to talk.

Director: And what would you talk about?

Handsome: Well, I couldn't just dive right in and ask about what potential she sees in me and how she can help bring it out.

Director: You have to lead your way to the point?

Handsome: Yes. But how?

Director: Maybe you, after a suitable amount of time, talk about her potential.

Handsome: I tell her what I think she can be?

Director: You don't think that's a good idea?

Handsome: Sure I do. But how will I know about her potential?

Director: How do you know anyone's potential?

Handsome: Honestly? I generally don't. But maybe you can help.

Director: How?

Handsome: You're good at seeing people's potential.

Director: Why do you think that?

Handsome: Because friends of ours are always saying how you encouraged them to do things they didn't think they could do. And they did them.

Director: So you want me to find your potential mate's potential.

Handsome: Yes. But now that we're at it, why don't you tell me my potential?

Director: Oh, but it's not that simple.

Handsome: Sure it is! Tell me, Director.

Director: You promise you won't be upset?

Handsome: I promise.

Director: Then I'll tell you. I think you have the potential to find someone who can help rouse you to your potential.

Handsome: I have the potential to find my potential?

Director: That's not quite what I said. I think finding someone who can stir you is your way.

Handsome: But it's embarrassing! Shouldn't I be able to realize my own potential without being stirred? How did you realize yours?

Director: To the extent I have? It was in part through being stirred by others.

Handsome: But you think I only need one other, not many like you?

Director: For the most part? Yes.

Handsome: Why?

Director: Because of the way you look.

13. HANDSOME, 2

Handsome: What do you mean?

Director: People are attracted to you. Yes?

Handsome: Yes.

Director: When they're attracted to you, what do they do?

Handsome: They find excuses to talk to me.

Director: And what do they talk about?

Handsome: Oh, it could be anything.

Director: Have any of them ever talked about your potential?

Handsome: Sure.

Director: What did they say?

Handsome: They all said I can do whatever I want to do.

Director: Did you believe them?

Handsome: No. They were flattering me.

Director: That's interesting. But you know, I don't have that problem when I talk to people.

Handsome: They speak more honestly with you about your potential?

Director: I suppose. They often tell me, Oh, you can't do this; you can't do that.

Handsome: But you fight against what they tell you, right?

Director: Sometimes I do. But, believe it or not, sometimes I listen. And I ask myself, Why can't I do this? Why can't I do that?

Handsome: Why can't you?

Director: Mostly? Because I don't want to.

Handsome: But when people tell me that I can't do something, it makes me want to do it all that much more!

Director: How often do people tell you that you can't do something?

Handsome: Well, not very often.

Director: So if I told you that you'll never live up to your potential, it would make you want to?

Handsome: It would.

Director: But you'd know it was a trick. Do you like being tricked?

Handsome: Of course not.

Director: So you'd be inclined not to live up to your potential just to spite me?

Handsome: Well, this is a crazy example. Of course I want to live up to my potential.

Director: Can you trust those who merely admire you for your looks to tell you what that potential is?

Handsome: No.

Director: Who can you trust?

Handsome: Someone who's living up to her own potential herself.

14. TRUTH

Director: Do you think you'll find many people who live up to their potential?

Handsome: No. And if we're talking about all of their potential, I might be lucky to find only one.

Director: Yes. But let's back up a step. Why would you trust someone just because she's living up to her potential?

Handsome: Because she would know what it takes. And those who know what it takes would never lie to someone who truly wants to know what it takes.

Director: You want the truth.

Handsome: Yes. I want the truth and not the flattery I usually get.

Director: Do you think people would flatter you as much if you were merely handsome and not rich?

Handsome: No, I don't think they would.

Director: And don't many people consider being rich the ultimate in living up to your potential? I mean, what's greater than being rich — other than being good looking and rich?

Handsome: That's exactly why I need a mate who will tell me the truth.

Director: Someone who can see you for what you really are, beyond your money and looks?

Handsome: Yes.

Director: What if that someone is, well, not as good looking as you?

Handsome: Well, there has to be a certain sort of basic attraction. But I don't need to find a ravishing beauty.

Director: But what beauty is more ravishing than the beauty that can see you for what you are and tell you about it?

Handsome: You have a point.

Director: Yes, and I think there's another point to be made. When someone sees you for what you are, what part of her does she use?

Handsome: I don't understand.

Director: Does she use her ears?

Handsome: She listens to me, so yes.

Director: Does she use her eyes?

Handsome: Of course.

Director: What about her mouth?

Handsome: You mean in the words that come out of it when she asks me questions and so on?

Director: Yes.

Handsome: Then, yes, she uses her mouth to help her understand me for what I am.

Director: If you found a woman who had great potential in ears, eyes, and mouth — would you be intrigued? Or would you only be intrigued if she was already living up to her potential in these things?

Handsome: I suppose I would be intrigued by both.

15. CHOICE

Director: But which would you choose to spend time with?

Handsome: I'd spend time with both.

Director: But if you had to choose one of them as a mate? Which would you choose?

Handsome: Assuming either one of them would have me? I don't know.

Director: Why don't you know?

Handsome: Because of this. If I pick the one already living up to her potential in these things — I would feel at a disadvantage.

Director: Why?

Handsome: Because I don't believe I'm living up to my potential in them.

Director: But what if she could help teach you?

Handsome: Yes, but then what's my role in the relationship? Student. I'd never feel myself to be an equal.

Director: So would you therefore choose the one who has yet to live up to her potential in these things?

Handsome: I'm inclined to say yes.

Director: Tell me why, exactly.

Handsome: Because we would learn together. Learn from each other.

Director: And therefore be equals.

Handsome: Yes.

Director: But what happens if you're wrong?

Handsome: What do you mean?

Director: What if you think she has more potential than she does?

Handsome: You mean she's about as good as she's going to get?

Director: Yes.

Handsome: Well, that's a problem.

Director: Why?

Handsome: Because we won't have much room to grow together.

Director: And growing together is a part of every healthy love?

Handsome: Definitely. And I'd even go so far as to say that growing together is the ultimate in common interest. In fact, it's hard to see what else could keep love alive.

16. Growing

Director: Tell me, Handsome. What is it that grows when you're growing together with your love? Does it all have to do with just ears, eyes, and mouth?

Handsome: It has to do with all of you.

Director: All of you as in heart, and soul, and mind?

Handsome: Yes, and those things determine how you'll use your ears, eyes, and mouth.

Director: So let me ask you this. What if there were two lovers who, before they met, had reached their potential in heart, soul, and mind? Couldn't they form a lasting relationship based not on what they might become, but on what they already are?

Handsome: But what do they do? Just sit around and admire one another? I don't believe people can somehow just reach their potential in these things and then that's it, they're done.

Director: But you seemed to think it's possible for someone to live up to her potential just a few moments ago.

Handsome: I was wrong.

Director: And you're objecting now because it's clear to you that there's always room to grow?

Handsome: Yes. Always.

Director: But some have more room than others?

Handsome: No, I'm not sure that's true. I mean, who's to say just how far someone can grow? Do you know what I mean?

Director: Yes, you mean that there's no absolute limit to growth.

Handsome: Exactly.

Director: Then let me ask you a hard question.

Handsome: By all means.

Director: What if you've grown as much as you can — with someone?

Handsome: And someone else comes along and you feel you can grow more with that person?

Director: Yes. What do you do?

Handsome: You're right that this is a hard question. What do you think you should do?

Director: Well, how would you feel if someone told you she's leaving you for another because you don't help her grow anymore?

Handsome: I would feel awful.

Director: But would you let her go?

Handsome: I would.

17. Saving It

Director: Then would you expect her to let you go if you're the one not growing?

Handsome: Ultimately? Yes. But first I would do everything possible to save the relationship.

Director: You mean you'd try to find ways for her to help you grow?

Handsome: Yes.

Director: But what if she simply can't? Would you still try to save things?

Handsome: She really can't? But maybe it's my fault. Maybe I'm not growing because I'm not appreciating her truly.

Director: True appreciation can make you grow?

Handsome: Of course.

Director: Then how will you come to appreciate her?

Handsome: I don't know.

Director: Will you blame yourself for not knowing?

Handsome: Ignorance deserves blame, don't you think?

Director: Usually. But what if there's simply nothing more that you can do?

Handsome: There's always something more that you can do.

Director: I know you believe that, and I think there's truth to it — but what if that 'something more' is best done by someone else?

Handsome: You mean I'd be doing her a disservice by keeping her tied to me?

Director: Yes.

Handsome: Then we'd go our separate ways.

18. Attraction, 2

Director: But now I'm wondering. Could we have gotten it all wrong?

Handsome: What do you mean?

Director: What if love isn't about growth?

Handsome: Then what would it be about?

Director: Strong attraction.

Handsome: But how can that be true? I feel strong attraction for different people almost every day!

Director: Yes, but if you fall deeply and truly in love with someone, the ultimate in strong attraction — do you think your other attractions will go away?

Handsome: Honestly? I don't know. I've always had these attractions.

Director: Do you think these attractions are love?

Handsome: Not true love.

Director: Then what are they?

Handsome: You want me to say they're lust.

Director: No, I want you to tell me how they seem to you.

Handsome: They seem like friendship.

Director: Friendship? Really?

Handsome: Yes.

Director: And you just want to be friends with those you're strongly attracted to? That's it?

Handsome: Well, you have a point. I want to be more than friends with them.

Director: You want to be lovers?

Handsome: Yes.

Director: If you have deep and true love, does it make any sense to sacrifice it in order to secure a fleeting romance?

Handsome: No, of course it doesn't. But what if it's not like that? What if the love was never really deep and true?

Director: Would a love affair make up for that lack?

Handsome: No, there's no substitute for deep and true love.

Director: Then it seems you need to find the real thing.

19. THE INTIMACY OF GROWTH

Handsome: I agree. But now I have an idea.

Director: Oh?

Handsome: What if we didn't have it all wrong?

Director: What do you mean?

Handsome: What if what we were saying about love and growth is true?

Director: You mean to say that love really is all about growth?

Handsome: Yes. But what if we're putting too much pressure on the relationship?

Director: How so?

Handsome: The way to growth might not always come through our mate.

Director: Can you elaborate?

Handsome: Sure. What if I have a friend, a very good friend, with whom I can grow?

Director: What if?

Handsome: Isn't that a good way to supplement growth at home?

Director: You're saying you have real love with your mate, you grow with her. But you also grow with your friend?

Handsome: Yes.

Director: Well, I think that sounds fine. But you have to make sure you've got the right mate.

Handsome: In what sense?

Director: What do you think she'll think about your growing with your friend?

Handsome: I don't know. What do you think she'll think?

Director: One of two things. One, she'll be pleased to see you grow. Two, she'll think her place has been taken by another.

Handsome: You mean she'll be jealous.

Director: Yes. And if she is, do you know why?

Handsome: Because growing together is one of the most intimate things you can do.

Director: Right. Now let's look at it another way. How would you feel if she turned to a friend for growth?

Handsome: I'd feel it's healthy. I'd be glad.

Director: But what if she turned to a friend because she's wholly stopped growing with you?

20. The End

Handsome: Well, that's a problem.

Director: A big enough problem for you to end the relationship?

Handsome: She never grows with me? Ever? Yes, that's a big enough problem.

Director: Even if you're still growing with her? And she's still wants to be with you?

Handsome: Why would she want to be with me? Growth has to be reciprocal or the relationship doesn't work.

Director: So let's say your mate isn't growing with a friend. And she's not growing with you.

Handsome: She's not growing at all?

Director: Right. And neither are you.

Handsome: What are you talking about?

Director: You've reached the end of growth — reciprocally. Would that work?

Handsome: Of course not.

Director: Not even if reaching the end of growth means reaching your potential?

Handsome: I thought we agreed there's always room to grow.

Director: Maybe we were wrong. Maybe we were confusing something.

Handsome: What do you mean?

Director: Couldn't it be that after we reach our potential, it takes an effort to sustain it? If so, we may have been confusing that sustaining effort with further growth. Do you see what I mean?

Handsome: Yes, I think I see. Though I'm not sure I like the idea. But tell me. If we reach our potential and we're working to sustain it, are we happy?

Director: Living life to the fullest of your potential with someone you love? I think most people would say that's the very definition of happiness.

Handsome: True.

Director: So what will you do?

Handsome: I'll find my love and we'll work together toward reaching our potential.

Director: And when you've reached it?

Handsome: If we reach it? We'll celebrate — and do everything we can not to let what we've accomplished slip away.

21. Growth Defined

Director: Now, you know there are those who will disagree with us.

Handsome: On what?

Director: On whether it's okay for growth ever to stop.

Handsome: I'm not even sure if it's okay for growth to stop.

Director: Yes, but maybe we're not talking about the same thing.

Handsome: What do you mean?

Director: I mean, let's define growth.

Handsome: Growth is learning.

Director: That's a bit different than what I had in mind.

Handsome: What did you have in mind?

Director: Growth is an increase in our power.

Handsome: Power? Are you talking about political power, financial power, and so on?

Director: No, I just mean the power of the individual.

Handsome: What, like being powerfully assertive or powerfully restrained?

Director: Yes.

Handsome: Well, that makes good sense. Though instead of talking about an increase in power we can simply say you learn to be more assertive or restrained.

Director: Yes, that's true. But here's the question. With these sorts of things, isn't there a limit? In other words, don't we eventually reach our peak? Or do you think we can go on growing indefinitely in assertiveness and restraint?

Handsome: No, you can only be so assertive, so restrained. So I think there's a limit, a natural limit.

Director: And what about the other sense of growth, your sense? Do you think there's a limit to how much we can learn?

Handsome: No.

Director: Tell me how learning would never end.

Handsome: That's easy. There's always something new to learn about. New facts. New people. New locations. New languages.

Director: And learning about these things can help you grow as a person?

Handsome: Yes. Everything you learn can help you grow.

Director: Okay. But now can you tell me how learning might end, aside from what we said about assertiveness and restraint?

Handsome: I don't see how it would.

Director: Well, let me ask you this. Do you think we can come to know ourselves?

Handsome: You mean, learn all there is to learn about ourselves?

Director: Yes. What do you think?

Handsome: I think it's possible.

Director: But now we're on controversial ground again.

Handsome: Why do you say that?

Director: Because there are those who would say there's always something more to learn about ourselves.

Handsome: Then it's never possible to know ourselves in full.

Director: That's the point.

Handsome: No, that's ridiculous. Of course it's possible to know ourselves fully.

Director: And if it's possible to know ourselves fully, is it possible to know another that way?

Handsome: Yes, I think it is.

Director: And in a relationship in which this has happened, when we each know ourselves and the other in full, growth, in the sense of learning about ourselves, is at an end?

Handsome: That kind of growth, yes. But that's when you turn outward to learning other things.

22. OUTWARD

Director: You turn to the things that involve learning without end.

Handsome: Yes. Together you learn new facts, explore new places, study new languages. And so on.

Director: But, Handsome, we're talking about love. Do you need love to engage in this kind of learning?

Handsome: No. But isn't it sweeter if you have it?

Director: Yes, I think you have a point. And what about with the other type of learning, learning about ourselves? Is that, too, sweeter with love?

Handsome: Of course.

Director: Now tell me. In learning about our love, our mate, won't there be some things we come to appreciate and some things we don't?

Handsome: Yes, we're only human, after all.

Director: If as you learn about your love you find that there are many more things to appreciate than you had thought — how do you feel?

Handsome: You feel deeper and deeper in love.

Director: And if as you learn you find that there are many more things you don't appreciate?

Handsome: You probably feel less in love.

Director: So what about the outward turn?

Handsome: What about it?

Director: If a couple feels less in love with each other, might they not turn outward in order to hide the fact that they're less in love?

Handsome: I think that happens every day.

Director: Does it work?

Handsome: Not really. Yes, the outward turn is a distraction from the ugly fact of the lessened love. But you can't hide something like that.

Director: Yes. But can't two people enjoy outward things — vacations, and so on — without being deeply in love?

Handsome: Of course they can.

Director: And might they not enjoy these things together as friends?

Handsome: Yes.

Director: But it's better if in addition to friendship there's love?

Handsome: But, Director, we love our friends.

Director: Just not in the way we love someone we're in love with?

Handsome: Yes. Just not in that way.

23. Friends And Wholes

Director: What's the difference between love for a friend and what we can call romantic love?

Handsome: I think there's a fair amount of overlap.

Director: The love we feel for a friend can be felt for someone we love romantically?

Handsome: Yes.

Director: But not all of the love we feel for a romantic love is felt for a friend.

Handsome: Correct.

Director: What is that part that we don't feel for a friend?

Handsome: Well, there's the physical attraction.

Director: Is that all that makes romantic love romantic love? The physical?

Handsome: No, of course not.

Director: What else is there that makes it what it is?

Handsome: Being in love.

Director: And what does that mean?

Handsome: Don't pretend you don't know what that means.

Director: It means you act foolishly?

Handsome: No.

Director: It means you want to buy chocolates and flowers for your love?

Handsome: You want me to tell you what it is? Fine. It's the feeling that you're made whole.

Director: Ah, an ancient definition. But doesn't that assume one thing?

Handsome: What thing?

Director: That you're not fully yourself without the other.

Handsome: Yes, and that's a good assumption.

Director: And if you're not fully yourself, you can't come to know yourself fully?

Handsome: Well, yes.

Director: So you only truly come to know yourself when you're with someone who makes you whole.

Handsome: It's not just 'someone', Director. It has to be The One.

Director: Of course. But let's be sure what this means. Are we certain that those who never find their One never come to know themselves?

Handsome: I don't like to say that. Maybe it's possible to come to know yourself on your own. But I think it takes a special kind of person.

Director: Yes, I agree. But do these special people lose their desire for a One once they know themselves fully?

Handsome: Why would they?

Director: Because they're already whole. Or do you think you can know yourself fully without being whole?

Handsome: No, you'd have to be whole. But I don't think that makes you lose your desire for your One.

Director: What kind of One would someone who's already whole want?

Handsome: A One that's whole, too.

Director: And what do you think they'd make?

Handsome: What do you mean?

Director: Can two wholes make one whole?

Handsome: Maybe they make a greater whole.

Director: Yes. But what about friendship? Can two wholes be friends?

Handsome: Certainly two wholes can be friends.

Director: Can two halves be friends?

Handsome: Yes.

Director: Can four quarters be friends?

Handsome: Yes, and I'd even say they can make a whole.

Director: A whole?

Handsome: A whole of friendship. It happens all the time.

24. WINGS

Director: You surprise me, Handsome. You're saying there are two types of whole?

Handsome: Don't you think it's true?

Director: I don't know. This runs counter to received wisdom, doesn't it?

Handsome: So what if it does? The question is only whether it's true.

Director: So if I make a whole of friendship with someone, that means I'm complete?

Handsome: Complete as far as friendship goes.

Director: But there's more to romantic wholeness? You're more complete with romantic love than with the love of friendship?

Handsome: Of course.

Director: But what more is there? Are you sure it's not just the physical aspect?

Handsome: No, I think it's more than that.

Director: What then?

Handsome: Have you ever heard that love makes the wings of your soul grow?

Director: Yes, I have. And that's another ancient notion.

Handsome: Well, that's what separates romantic love from the love of friends — wings.

Director: And what do wings let us do?

Handsome: Soar.

Director: Soar for the sake of soaring, or soar for the sake of something else?

Handsome: If you've ever soared, you know that it's always soaring for the sake of soaring.

Director: Well, it's hard to argue with that. So romantic love makes us soar.

Handsome: Yes, it does.

Director: And that's what distinguishes it from friendship.

Handsome: Right.

Director: Friendship is earth bound.

Handsome: You mean with a good friend you have your feet firmly planted on the ground?

Director: That's what I mean. Is it true?

Handsome: It's true.

Director: Isn't it good to have your feet planted firmly on the ground?

Handsome: Of course it is. But it's always better if you can fly.

25. FLEETING LOVE

Director: So the love of friends makes you find your feet, while the love of a lover makes you grow your wings.

Handsome: A lover? You make it sound as if there can be more than one!

Director: Excuse me if I've offended you, Handsome. But haven't you had more than one love in your time?

Handsome: Yes. But it's only The One who'll make you grow wings.

Director: And you haven't found your One.

Handsome: No, I haven't.

Director: But you're certain you've been in love?

Handsome: As certain as can be.

Director: And none of this love grew your wings?

Handsome: You're asking if I've ever soared?

Director: Yes.

Handsome: I've plummeted from a height. But I've never yet soared.

Director: Remarkable. How did you happen upon the height?

Handsome: I climbed a mountain to meet my fleeting love. And then I fell.

Director: I'm sorry to hear it. But your mention of your fleeting love makes me wonder. Are there basically three sorts of love? Fleeting love, love of friends, and love of The One?

Handsome: Yes, I think that's right.

Director: Are you sure there are no other types of love?

Handsome: Well, there's love of family. But for our purposes it's basically the same as the love of true friends.

Director: Then are we right to divide all these sorts of love into two types? Romantic — fleeting love and love of The One; and non-romantic — love of family and friends?

Handsome: Yes, we are.

Director: Alright. So tell me. What's characteristic about fleeting romantic love?

Handsome: You want for there to be wholeness. You want it very badly. But the fit isn't quite right. It's close. Close enough that you might madly attempt to make it work. But it's just no good.

Director: And the sooner you figure that out the better?

Handsome: The sooner the better.

Director: So why climb a mountain for a fleeting lover?

Handsome: Because sometimes you don't know if it's a true match until you do.

Director: If the match is true you soar, and if it's not you plummet?

Handsome: Yes. Just like the man who flew too close to the sun.

26. MELTING

Director: But do you know the story, Handsome? There was a man whose wings were made of wax. He flew too close to the sun. The wax melted. And he fell into the sea and drowned.

Handsome: Of course I know the story. I'm the one who brought it up.

Director: Well, what if he didn't drown?

Handsome: What do you mean?

Director: I mean, that's the truth of the story — the whole story. He didn't drown.

Handsome: He just swam in the sea?

Director: Yes, he swam in the sea and was picked up by sailors who took him to the blessed isles.

Handsome: You're making this up.

Director: It's a myth, right? What's wrong with making some of it up as you go?

Handsome: But you seem to want to prove that fleeting love is somehow good.

Director: Well, if you learn from it — isn't it?

Handsome: Yes, I suppose — because it will prepare you for true love.

Director: And our man found true love in the blessed isles and lived happily ever after. There. What do you think?

Handsome: I wish it were true.

Director: It's as true as any myth ever was true.

Handsome: So what do the sailors represent in the myth?

Director: Someone who knows a thing or two about the sea of love. Namely? Me.

Handsome: So you're going to take me across the sea to the blessed isles where I'll find love, true love that will make me whole and grow my wings?

Director: That's the idea. And this time the wings won't be made of wax.

27. Sun

Handsome: What will they be made with?

Director: If we're talking about the true love that makes you whole? Knowledge.

Handsome: And if we're not talking about that kind of love?

Director: Wax.

Handsome: And are you saying that knowledge won't melt if I get too close to the sun?

Director: The funny thing about knowledge is that it grows stronger as you get closer to the sun.

Handsome: So what's the sun a metaphor for?

Director: Well, two things. Being, being eternally the same. And becoming, coming to be, change.

Handsome: How can it be both?

Director: It all depends on your wings. If you fly by means of knowledge, the sun is pure being, eternal being. That means its light will strengthen your knowledge of your forever love and the two of you as a never ending whole, a whole that existed before all time.

Handsome: So fleeting lovers never experience that kind of sun.

Director: No, they don't. Though it would be good if they could.

Handsome: Why?

Director: Because in the awesomely bright light of the sun of being they'd come to know quite clearly what sort of love they've got. Best to know that sooner rather than later.

Handsome: But what about when the sun is becoming, coming to be, change?

Director: Something interesting happens here. The becoming is the fleeting, right? That which isn't eternal but is always coming to be. Given this, it would be best if fleeting lovers could fly straight to the sun — and hurl themselves in.

Handsome: That seems harsh. Why would they want to do that?

Director: Because the sun of becoming is good for all things fleeting, even if it burns them up. When that happens they're reborn and made ready for another go.

Handsome: In which case they'll fly straight into the sun of becoming once more?

Director: In all likelihood? Yes, at least a few more times.

Handsome: But wouldn't their wax melt before they got there each time?

Director: Well, that's a very good question. I've often wondered about that. Can we be saying there must be at least some knowledge in their wings in order for them to reach the sun of becoming without falling into the sea? What do you think?

Handsome: But if they have knowledge, is it fleeting knowledge? Is there such a thing?

Director: Have you ever known something but forgotten?

Handsome: Of course.

Director: That's what fleeting knowledge is.

Handsome: I see. But now I'm wondering. Couldn't true love go well with both aspects of the sun?

Director: How might that be?

Handsome: On the one hand we have our eternal wholeness. On the other hand we have learning and growing and whatever other good things that are associated with change, with coming to be, with becoming. And, in fact, our wholeness itself is a change, is a coming to be from when we're not whole, even though the wholeness we achieve partakes of the eternal. So that means wholeness itself requires both types of sun.

Director: That's an admirable explanation, my friend. An admirable job.

28. What It Is

Handsome: Thanks. But I think that's enough with this metaphor.

Director: Has it answered all your questions?

Handsome: Ha! Hardly.

Director: What would you like to know?

Handsome: It's one thing to say love gives you wings, or makes you whole, or whatever. But it's another thing altogether to say what love actually is, and not what it does.

Director: Love is a connection between two people.

Handsome: Sure, we can say that. But you can have a connection with an enemy.

Director: Haven't you ever heard of loving your enemy?

Handsome: I have. But I've never understood why you'd want to do that.

Director: Then why don't we say that love is a connection between two people, excluding enemies?

Handsome: You can't be serious.

Director: Why not?

Handsome: Because think of all the connections you have in your life!

Director: And you can't love them all?

Handsome: Of course you can't, not in any meaningful way.

Director: You're saying that love is exclusive.

Handsome: I am.

Director: It excludes all the people in the world except your fleeting loves or The One you love and your family and friends?

Handsome: Yes, though I'll concede that we can think of 'friends' in a very broad sense.

Director: Now, what about hate?

Handsome: What about it?

Director: Do you hate all those who aren't in your exclusive world?

Handsome: No, of course not.

Director: How do you feel toward them?

Handsome: For the most part? In all honesty? Indifferent.

Director: But sometimes hateful?

Handsome: I suppose that's true for some people, Director. But not for me.

29. HATE

Director: Tell me, Handsome. Do you agree it helps you to know a thing if you know its opposite?

Handsome: I do.

Director: Then if we know what hate is, we'll have a pretty good idea of what love is?

Handsome: Maybe.

Director: Well, what is hate?

Handsome: A very strong feeling of dislike.

Director: Does that mean love is a very strong feeling of liking?

Handsome: Yes, I think it does.

Director: When you dislike someone very strongly, what do you want to do?

Handsome: What do you want to do? I suppose you want to harm them.

Director: And if you like someone strongly?

Handsome: You want to help.

Director: When you want to harm someone, do you have to know how to harm them, or can you harm them without knowing how?

Handsome: Generally speaking? You have to know how to harm them.

Director: And what about with helping someone? Do you have to know how?

Handsome: Yes, of course.

Director: So knowing is the key. Knowing how to help. Knowing how to harm.

Handsome: Yes, but before we go down that road I have to say that I'm not so sure.

Director: About what?

Handsome: About whether we should ever deliberately harm someone.

Director: But that's what someone who hates wants, isn't it?

Handsome: It is. But we shouldn't always do what we want.

Director: But we should always do what we want to do when it comes to love?

Handsome: Well, if we're talking about helping someone, yes.

Director: Then love and hate make for an interesting pair.

Handsome: How so?

Director: We bottle up our hate but let our love flow.

Handsome: I don't think bottling up hate is a good idea.

Director: Why not?

Handsome: Because one day it might explode.

Director: So what can we do? Learn not to hate?

Handsome: I'm not sure something like that can be learned.

Director: Because we can't help what we feel?

Handsome: That's right.

Director: I don't know, Handsome. What we think and what we feel seem to me to be closely linked. So if we change what we think, won't we change what we feel?

Handsome: Sure, Director. But if someone does you repeated harm — what's to think?

30. A Suggestion

Director: That makes me wonder.

Handsome: Oh? What are you wondering?

Director: If someone does us harm, and it's not a great harm, and it's only once — what might we feel?

Handsome: You mean as far as hate goes? Probably nothing.

Director: But if we did hate, might it not be like what we talked about with love?

Handsome: I'm not following.

Director: We talked about fleeting love. Is there such a thing as fleeting hate?

Handsome: You know, I think there is.

Director: Then might there be such a thing as a lasting hate, since we've been talking about lasting love, and love and hate are opposites?

Handsome: I know there's such a thing.

Director: But have you ever felt it?

Handsome: A lasting hate? No, I haven't.

Director: And you've yet to feel a lasting love, a lasting romantic love?

Handsome: True. But what are you suggesting?

Director: What does it seem I'm suggesting?

Handsome: You seem to me to be suggesting that if I can come to feel a lasting hate, I might discover how to feel a lasting love!

Director: No, I'm not suggesting that.

Handsome: Then what are you suggesting?

Director: That right now you and I seem to have no idea about either love or hate.

Handsome: What? Are you saying you've never felt a lasting love?

Director: Regardless of how I answer that question, one basic fact remains. I'm single, Handsome. So what do you think?

Handsome: Yes, but what about hate? Have you ever felt a lasting hate?

Director: Hate as a passion that gnaws and eats me up inside over time? No, I've never felt that.

Handsome: Then I guess you're right. How can we have any idea about hate or love?

31. INTENSE, OPPOSED

Director: Well, maybe we should explore a bit more. Have you heard of love / hate relationships?

Handsome: I have.

Director: What are they like?

Handsome: I think they consist of intense, opposed emotions.

Director: Can you think of other relationships that are like this, that have intense, opposed emotions?

Handsome: No, I can't.

Director: So is this evidence that the pairing of love and hate might be something unique in the world?

Handsome: Yes, but aren't we making a bad assumption?

Director: What assumption is that?

Handsome: That if you love you must hate, and if you hate you must love.

Director: No, we're not assuming that. There could be ninety-nine love relationships with no hate whatsoever, and then the hundredth comes round brimming periodically with hate.

Handsome: But then that means that only the hundredth relationship is unique in the sense that it has intense, opposed emotions.

Director: Maybe. Or maybe we could say that the hundredth made actual what is merely potential in all the other ninety-nine. But I don't like to say that.

Handsome: Neither do I. So I think we're heading down the wrong path. The ninety-nine don't have the potential for a love / hate relationship.

Director: Then what makes a couple have the potential?

Handsome: I think one or both of them would have to be unbalanced.

Director: What do you think typically makes someone unbalanced?

Handsome: Oh, I don't know. It could be many things. But usually? I'd say it's insecurity.

32. INSECURITY

Director: If you're insecure, how does your love seem to you?

Handsome: The love itself? Endangered.

Director: And if you feel it's endangered, how will you love?

Handsome: Desperately.

Director: And if you love desperately, what happens?

Handsome: The other might pull away.

Director: And if the other pulls away?

Handsome: I guess you feel wounded.

Director: How do we feel toward those who we think wound us?

Handsome: We resent them?

Director: And if we resent them, what do we sometimes do?

Handsome: We act out.

Director: How do we act out?

Handsome: We act out with spite.

Director: How far a step is it from spite to hate?

Handsome: Not very far, I suppose.

Director: And all this could be prevented by a bit of security?

Handsome: Yes, that's true.

Director: What makes for security?

Handsome: Trust that the other loves you.

Director: Loves you as one among many?

Handsome: No, of course not. Loves you exclusively.

Director: But what if your lover does love you exclusively, and yet you have doubts?

Handsome: Then the only one to blame for your troubles is you.

33. Balance

Director: So how do you avoid having a lover who's insecure?

Handsome: You look for someone with confidence.

Director: Someone who knows that you love her as much as she loves you?

Handsome: Well, yes.

Director: Why are you hesitating?

Handsome: Because it's rare to find that perfect balance of love.

Director: You mean the rule is that one side loves more than the other, and the exception is balance?

Handsome: Yes. Wouldn't you agree?

Director: That often seems the way of it. But I'm not sure which is the rule and which the exception.

Handsome: Oh? Why not?

Director: Because we're suggesting imbalance leads to trouble, no?

Handsome: Yes, certainly.

Director: Do most couples have trouble? I'm not talking about little spats here and there. I'm talking about real, systematic trouble in the relationship. Foundational trouble.

Handsome: Yes, I see what you're getting at. If that kind of trouble were the rule, why would people want to get into these relationships in the first place?

Director: Because there are exceptions, if it's true that trouble is the rule.

Handsome: Yes, and those exceptions would make everyone else think they can be exceptions, too.

Director: So what would you have them do, the ones who think they can be exceptions but can't?

Handsome: I'd have them save themselves a world of trouble and avoid relationships that are doomed from the start to fail.

34. JEALOUSY

Director: But this is ridiculous, Handsome.

Handsome: Why?

Director: First of all, it's no small thing to say that so many people should stay out of relationships. Can't you see that?

Handsome: Of course I can see that. But why else do you object?

Director: Because how would the ones who do form loving couples, the exceptions, if we're right that they're exceptions — how would they feel if they're such a great minority?

Handsome: I think they'd feel honored. And wouldn't people honor them?

Director: Some might. But I'm not sure about the rest.

Handsome: Why not?

Director: Because some people will be jealous.

Handsome: Jealous that they can't be exceptions, too?

Director: Yes, and then what do you think they'll do?

Handsome: They'll say to themselves, I can be an exception, too! And they'll rush headlong into fleeting love and try to make it last.

Director: True. And they might not even rush into fleeting love. They might rush into whatever is at hand, love or not. But that's not the worst of it.

Handsome: What is?

Director: Don't you know? Some of the jealous will try to interfere with the relationships that work.

Handsome: You mean by lying and spreading malicious gossip and so on.

Director: Of course.

Handsome: The thinking is, if I can't have something good, no one else can either?

Director: Don't you think that's how some people think?

Handsome: I do.

Director: Then we must find ways to protect ourselves from them.

35. PROTECTION

Handsome: What do you have in mind?

Director: What's the best remedy for jealousy's poison?

Handsome: Truth.

Director: So if our lovers tell the truth to each other, that's enough?

Handsome: Well, I'm not sure that's enough.

Director: Why not?

Handsome: Because the poison affects others, too.

Director: It affects the good opinion others have of the lovers?

Handsome: Yes, and that eventually comes to harm the lovers themselves.

Director: So what if our lovers go on the offensive?

Handsome: What do you mean?

Director: What if they tell the truth about the poisoners?

Handsome: What truth will they tell?

Director: The reason why they do what they do.

Handsome: Jealousy? But that's what people always say the reason is.

Director: But does that make it any less true?

Handsome: No. But I don't think this is a good way for our lovers to protect themselves. It doesn't stop the jealous from doing what they do.

Director: What can be done to stop them?

Handsome: Nothing, I'm afraid.

Director: So, really, all the lovers have is the truth they tell each other?

Handsome: Yes, and that means they have to believe each other. And that's the only way.

36. DOUBT

Director: If they believe one another, that means they don't doubt each other. Right?

Handsome: Right.

Director: But what about the jealous ones? Do you think they believe one another? Or do you think it more likely they'd doubt?

Handsome: I think it's very much more likely they'd doubt.

Director: Why?

Handsome: Because they spread lies. And they assume that everyone else does, too. So they don't trust anyone.

Director: But honest people might trust them?

Handsome: Yes, they might. And then they'll believe the lies.

Director: And there's nothing we can do about this?

Handsome: Well, we'd have to get the honest people to see our lovers with their own eyes, see them acting in ways that expose the lies.

Director: And when the honest see the truth, they'll know the jealous for what they are?

Handsome: Eventually? Yes.

Director: So what happens then?

Handsome: One of two things. One, the honest will break off relations with the jealous. This is if they're strong.

Director: And two, if they're weak?

Handsome: They'll value their relationships with the liars enough to keep them intact — which means they're well on their way to becoming liars themselves.

37. Love, Relationships

Director: Lies are contagious, yes. But your mention of relationships has got me wondering again.

Handsome: About what?

Director: About the difference between relationships and love.

Handsome: Tell me what you think.

Director: Well, on the one hand you can have love without a relationship. Yes?

Handsome: Yes, I agree.

Director: But on the other hand you can have a relationship without love. No?

Handsome: Of course. People have all sorts of loveless relationships.

Director: So you can have love without a relationship and you can have a relationship without love. Just as you can have a relationship with love. In other words, anything's possible?

Handsome: I suppose that's true.

Director: Yes, that's what I supposed. But now I'm not so sure.

Handsome: Why not?

Director: I don't know that you can have love without a relationship.

Handsome: Why?

Director: Because what if it's true that love always finds a way?

Handsome: If I didn't know you better I'd say you're becoming a romantic!

Director: What about you? Do you believe love always finds a way?

Handsome: Honestly? I do.

Director: Then humor me with an example. Suppose you're in a night club, dancing away. And you fall in love with a beautiful woman dancing nearby. And she falls in love with you. And so you dance with one another. And your love grows deeper as the night goes on. Is such a love possible, or am I talking nonsense?

Handsome: No, it's possible.

Director: Okay. But do you have a relationship?

Handsome: We spend the whole night dancing?

Director: The whole night, into the early morning hours.

Handsome: And we never talk.

Director: No, not a word. Is it a relationship?

Handsome: It is, of sorts — though a lot of people would disagree.

Director: Well, let's not get too worried about who agrees with what. The important thing is that love is starting to find a way. Yes?

Handsome: Yes.

Director: So here's what I want to know. Suppose at the end of the night you finally get to talk. And you realize immediately that she's telling you lies. What does that do to your relationship?

Handsome: It ruins it.

Director: Why?

Handsome: Because I wouldn't lie to her.

38. INTEGRITY

Director: Why wouldn't you lie to her? She lied to you.

Handsome: Sure. But if I don't have my integrity, then what have I got?

Director: You need a woman who values her integrity as much as you do yours.

Handsome: Yes.

Director: Is that the secret formula for a good relationship?

Handsome: I think it is.

Director: But how many people really have integrity? Is it most?

Handsome: Honestly? I don't know. But I think there are a lot of people of integrity out there.

Director: Then why are there so few good relationships?

Handsome: Are you suggesting there aren't many people of integrity?

Director: Wouldn't that explain the lack of good relationships?

Handsome: Yes, I suppose it would. But we could also explain it by saying that integrity and attraction don't always go together.

Director: You mean you might meet someone of integrity but not be attracted to her.

Handsome: Right.

Director: And you think that sort of thing happens very often?

Handsome: Often enough to make for a lack of strong relationships.

Director: Interesting. And maybe people go about it all the wrong way.

Handsome: How do they go about it?

Director: They set out looking for someone they're attracted to and then, when they find such a person, they hope that integrity will happen to be there, too.

Handsome: When what they should do is set out for integrity and hope attraction will be there, too?

Director: Yes. Don't you think that makes more sense?

Handsome: I'm inclined to say it does.

Director: But that's not what you do, is it?

Handsome: True, but I'm open to persuasion.

Director: Good.

39. At First Sight

Handsome: But there's a problem I can't seem to get around.

Director: Oh?

Handsome: When I walk into a room I know right away who's the most beautiful looking. And if I spend five minutes talking to her, I know if I'm attracted or not.

Director: But you don't know about her integrity.

Handsome: Right. It generally takes time to figure out whether someone has that.

Director: And you can't afford the time.

Handsome: Now you're making me feel ashamed.

Director: What's to be ashamed of, Handsome? You want to be able to walk into a room and see at a glance who has integrity and who doesn't.

Handsome: I know that's not possible. But you see the dilemma, don't you?

Director: Yes, and a terrible dilemma it is.

Handsome: So what can I do?

Director: You might be doomed to talk to all of the attractive women, taking your time with them, getting to know them, and ruling out all of those who have no integrity.

Handsome: But when I find one who has it?

Director: That's when you pounce.

Handsome: But she'll want to know if I have integrity.

Director: Just be yourself and I'm sure you'll be fine.

Handsome: And what do we do once we've confirmed we're attracted to one another and have integrity in common?

Director: What do you do? If I didn't know better, I'd say you were rather inexperienced in these things.

Handsome: But I am inexperienced — in finding lasting love.

Director: I can see you're in earnest. Well, let things take their natural course. Do what we said. Learn together. Grow together. Make each other whole. Sprout your wings. And, most of all, just enjoy one another's company.

Handsome: And if we can do those things, we're the lucky ones — the exceptions to the rule?

Director: If you can do those things, you're the lucky ones — regardless of any rule.

40. DIRECTOR

Handsome: But what about you?

Director: What about me?

Handsome: Don't you want to be an exception?

Director: You're asking if I want lasting love?

Handsome: Yes. After all, you have all the qualities it takes. You have integrity — the hardest quality to have. And you're reasonably attractive, if you don't mind my speaking plainly.

Director: Thanks for the vote of confidence.

Handsome: Have you sought out women of integrity?

Director: I have, and I found a good many.

Handsome: And you weren't attracted to one of them romantically?

Director: Not a one.

Handsome: Why not?

Director: Why does a dolphin swim? I don't know.

Handsome: But you have been attracted to other women, right?

Director: Oh yes, certainly.

Handsome: But they lacked integrity?

Director: Here's the thing. I had no way of knowing.

Handsome: Why not?

Director: Let's just say I could only admire them from afar.

Handsome: But why not approach them?

Director: Something held me back.

Handsome: What?

Director: I couldn't say. It was just a feeling I had, a feeling that said to resist their charms.

Handsome: I think you've been foolish. Your life mate might have been one of those women!

Director: Yes, yes. It would be easy to take your point and be duly admonished. But I, for one, listen to my feelings.

Handsome: But what if one of those feelings is love?

Director: Are you suggesting attraction is love?

Handsome: No, of course not. There's more to it than that. But attraction is certainly a feeling. And you just said you listen to your feelings.

Director: But I'm not at all sure attraction is a feeling. Attraction seems to me to be more of a force. And aren't forces decidedly different than feelings, my friend?

41. FORCE

Handsome: But what if I say that feelings seem to me to be forces that operate on us?

Director: Forces like the force of attraction? You can say that. But I'm not sure it's true.

Handsome: Why not?

Director: Well, answer me honestly now. When you feel happy is that some force operating on you? The happiness force?

Handsome: Honestly? No, there's no happiness force.

Director: What about when you feel sad? Is that the sadness force at work?

Handsome: No.

Director: And so on, and so on? It's too simple an explanation to say that each feeling is the result of a particular force. Isn't it?

Handsome: I agree.

Director: But now what about the force of attraction? A force, yes?

Handsome: Just because you call it a force it doesn't mean that's what it is.

Director: Maybe physics will help. Do you know of the law of gravitation?

Handsome: Of course I know about the law of gravity.

Director: It amounts to a law of attraction of objects?

Handsome: Yes.

Director: Have you felt subject to this law when dealing with beautiful women?

Handsome: You mean I had no choice but to be attracted? I have.

Director: And there was something very real that drew you in?

Handsome: There was. And I suppose you want me to call it a force.

Director: Yes. Does happiness feel like this, feel like something that's pulling you in, or pushing you away, or whatever — a force that makes you happy?

Handsome: No, it doesn't.

Director: And what about sadness?

Handsome: No, there's no sadness force that pulls me in, or pushes me away, or whatever.

Director: And happiness and sadness are feelings?

Handsome: Yes, they are.

Director: But decidedly not forces, not forces in the same sense as in the force of attraction, a force that no doubt pulls you in?

Handsome: No, not in that sense at all. You've made your point.

Director: Yes. But somehow I feel we let go a bit too easily on what you were saying about feelings and forces. For instance, we might say attraction is an external force while feelings are internal forces. Or we might say feelings are the result of a great many external forces operating on a person, the combination of which amounts to happiness, or sadness, and so on. But let's take that up another time. For now, we'll just say that attraction is a force. And we need to know how to deal with it.

42. MASSIVE OBJECTS

Handsome: What's to deal with? You're either drawn in or not.

Director: But what draws what?

Handsome: What do you mean?

Director: Doesn't the more massive draw the less massive?

Handsome: Strictly speaking, they draw each other. But I know what you mean. The less massive goes toward the more massive more than the more massive goes toward the less massive.

Director: So if you're more drawn to someone than she is to you, you must be the less massive object of the two. Right?

Handsome: Right. And if others are more drawn to me than I am to them, I'm the more massive.

Director: Yes. Which do you think it's better to be?

Handsome: The more massive.

Director: And if you're always the more massive all sorts of would-be lovers will be attracted and hurtle toward you?

Handsome: Well, I'm not sure how good that sounds.

Director: So you'd rather be the less massive, drawn toward every more massive object that passes your way?

Handsome: I want to maintain my own course without the interference of any force.

Director: How will you do that? I mean, gravitation is a law. There's no way not to attract or be attracted, is there?

Handsome: Maybe I have to go where no one else is.

Director: No one else? Not even your lasting love?

Handsome: Look. Why don't we think of it like this? My lasting love and I will be like a binary star in which two stars orbit around their common center of mass.

Director: Two stars orbiting around what they have in common? That sounds good. But what if others come to orbit the two of you?

Handsome: Let them. My love and I will be queen and king and they will be our court.

43. ORBITING

Director: In that case you'll have to rule your hearts closely.

Handsome: Why?

Director: Why? You don't think there will be temptation in having others who are so attracted to you that they spend their lives orbiting you? After all, weren't you the one who said gravity works on each object, the lesser and the greater both?

Handsome: Well, yes, I can see what you mean. But I guess that's just something we'll have to live with.

Director: Yes. But let me ask you this. Do you and your love have to make up a binary star?

Handsome: What else could we be?

Director: Planet and moon.

Handsome: No, no. That's all wrong.

Director: Why?

Handsome: Because if I'm a planet, I'm orbiting a star. I'm attracted to the star. And if my lover is orbiting me as my moon, well, then I'm not orbiting her.

Director: So it's a binary star or nothing?

Handsome: It's that or nothing for me.

44. MASS

Director: So what does it take to create that common center you're talking about?

Handsome: Well, I have to admit — I don't know much about astrophysics.

Director: Then let's forget about the star metaphor. What do you want to have in common with your love?

Handsome: I want our masses to be as nearly equal as can be.

Director: Okay. But what makes up the attraction mass of a human being?

Handsome: I think it's two things — heart and mind.

Director: Are you forgetting what we're calling the physical?

Handsome: Well, that too.

Director: So there are three areas of mass. And their total mass is what attracts you to someone.

Handsome: Assuming I'm not more massive when it comes to these things.

Director: Yes, of course. But suppose, for a minute, that you're not the more massive one, that you meet someone with greater mass. What then?

Handsome: As we've said, I'll be attracted.

Director: And does it work like this? Let's say you meet a woman who has a mass of one hundred in heart and one hundred in mind, but only two or three when it comes to looks, to the physical. Attracted?

Handsome: Well, that depends on my mass.

Director: So if you've got a mass of seventy-five in heart, seventy-five in mind, and seventy-five in body — what then?

Handsome: Her total mass is 202 or 203 while mine is 225. She's attracted to me.

Director: But are the masses close enough, nearly equal enough, to give you what you need?

Handsome: Possibly.

Director: Okay. But what if she's only attracted to someone who has a mass of one hundred in both heart and mind, just like her?

Handsome: You're telling me that if, for instance, someone with masses of ninety in heart and mind and a physical mass of one hundred comes along, she won't be attracted?

Director: Nope. No attraction.

Handsome: We're talking about a total of 202 or 203 to a total of 280. I think there's going to be some attraction, Director.

Director: I don't know, my friend. Some people know what they want.

Handsome: You can know all you want. But when the force of attraction starts to draw you in, it's funny how your mind can change.

45. The Ideal

Director: Yes, I know what you mean. But you really don't think people can hold out for an ideal?

Handsome: You mean they fight the attraction?

Director: I prefer to say they resist.

Handsome: Well, if they do they'd be foolish to hold out for the perfect ideal.

Director: What's the perfect ideal?

Handsome: Exact matches in all three areas.

Director: What are the odds of finding these perfect matches?

Handsome: Long — too long.

Director: Someone could go a whole lifetime without finding them?

Handsome: Easily.

Director: So if you're going to hold out, it's more practical to hold out for just one or two of the three categories?

Handsome: Yes.

Director: Which category are you holding out for?

Handsome: Me? I'm not holding out for an ideal. I'm just looking for someone with as close a total mass to mine as I can find.

Director: Really? And if that someone has a very strong body and mind, but not so strong a heart?

Handsome: Well....

Director: I think you're holding out for heart, Handsome.

Handsome: What if I am?

Director: It means you won't be happy unless you find someone with a heart as strong as your own.

Handsome: How strong do you think my heart is?

Director: What, you want a number? I don't think it's a good idea for me to give you one.

Handsome: Why not?

Director: Because we've been speaking as if there's a science to all of this, a physics based on objective numbers.

Handsome: And there isn't?

Director: No, of course not. The masses of heart, body, and mind are each open to subjective interpretation.

Handsome: To a certain degree.

Director: You mean everyone basically agrees as to who has what kind of heart, or body, or mind?

Handsome: Don't they?

Director: I don't know that they do.

46. A Model

Handsome: Well, there's a way to find out.

Director: How?

Handsome: We can use a rating system where everyone rates everyone else.

Director: What good will that do?

Handsome: It will show us quite clearly how far people agree. And we'll make it so that each of our three traits can bring a maximum score of one hundred. So there's no inflation. No one can say someone has, for instance, a mind of one thousand. A total of three hundred is the most someone can have.

Director: Okay. But rating people is one thing. Getting what you want is another.

Handsome: What if we let the ratings take care of that?

Director: What do you mean?

Handsome: Your average scores will tell you who's your match, or will at least narrow the field significantly.

Director: Love by average? I don't think I like it. In fact, I think your whole rating model is flawed and needs to be replaced.

Handsome: Why?

Director: First of all, if someone thinks you've got a heart of a million, do you really want to tell her she has to limit herself to a hundred?

Handsome: Well.... Honestly? If it were me? No, I'd want the million.

Director: Yes. Who wouldn't? And the model is flawed in another way, a fundamental way.

Handsome: How?

Director: I think it's fine to work with points. But we shouldn't use them to rate people.

Handsome: What should we do with them?

Director: Use them to secure our mate.

Handsome: And how do we do that?

Director: By making an offer with our points. If the other accepts, we have a deal.

Handsome: A business transaction? Ha! I think you're joking.

Director: Maybe I am. But hear me out on just one more thing. In this model we all have different amounts of points. Some more than three hundred, some less.

Handsome: And whoever has the most points wins?

Director: Provided he or she is willing to offer them up, yes.

Handsome: Well, that sounds fine. But we haven't talked about the most important thing. How do we get our points?

47. The Source

Director: We get them from what others think of our hearts, bodies, and minds.

Handsome: A sort of rating.

Director: Yes, but it's a private evaluation. It doesn't get averaged with the rest.

Handsome: So if we privately think someone totals a thousand, but she thinks we're only worth a hundred — no deal?

Director: And she actually thinks she's worth a thousand? No deal.

Handsome: But if she thinks she's only worth a hundred?

Director: Then we get what you might call a steal.

Handsome: I think that makes sense.

Director: Yes, but it gets a bit more complicated.

Handsome: How so?

Director: Are heart, body, and mind really the only sources of points?

Handsome: Well, there's one obvious thing we haven't talked about.

Director: Yes?

Handsome: Wealth.

Director: You mean people can be as attracted to wealth as they are to any of the other three categories?

Handsome: I do. And don't act surprised.

Director: And what about power?

Handsome: Political power and the like?

Director: Yes.

Handsome: That, too, can earn you points.

Director: And what about fame? More points?

Handsome: More points, for those with a taste for that sort of thing.

Director: So we have six categories now — mind, body, heart; wealth, power, fame. But there's something peculiar about our list.

Handsome: Oh? What?

Director: It seems that at least one of the first three is always involved in the acquisition of the last three.

Handsome: Can you say more?

Director: Mind, Handsome. How do people acquire wealth, power, and fame?

Handsome: They have to use their minds. Or, speaking strictly — their brains.

Director: Yes. But let's not worry about being too strict. And let's note one thing. Even if these people somehow inherited their wealth, power, or fame — they still have to use their minds if they want to maintain what they've been given.

Handsome: That's true.

Director: So do you see what this means?

Handsome: It means that mind is the most attractive feature a person can have, as far as these other things go.

Director: But do the people who crave wealth, power, and fame in a partner always see that?

Handsome: They almost never see it.

Director: If that's true, then why?

Handsome: Because all they can focus on is the wealth, power, and fame.

Director: They're dazzled?

Handsome: Yes.

Director: Then we should do what we can to help.

48. HELPING

Handsome: What can we do? Awe them with a demonstration of mind?

Director: Why not?

Handsome: And then they'll learn to fall in love with mind?

Director: Is that what you want them to do?

Handsome: It's better than the alternative.

Director: Then what sort of mind do you suppose will awe them best?

Handsome: One that's very powerful.

Director: And who will be awed?

Handsome: Those with less powerful minds.

Director: Is that who you'd like to impress?

Handsome: Me, personally? I don't want to be in the business of awing less powerful minds. I just want to impress the equal who's my mate.

Director: An equal who craves wealth, power, and fame?

Handsome: Are you suggesting that just because I'm a match intellectually and have the other things she wants, we'd make a good pair?

Director: Well, I don't know. She wants power and fame, Handsome.

Handsome: I've got some power and a modest bit of fame, you know.

Director: You might need more of each.

Handsome: But who says I want someone like this?

Director: You want someone who doesn't want money, power, and fame?

Handsome: Yes.

Director: But you have these things, in whatever degree.

Handsome: So the one I want won't want me because I have things she doesn't care for?

Director: In all likelihood? Yes.

Handsome: So what do I do?

Director: Forget about her. Educate her. Or get rid of the things in question.

49. EDUCATION

Handsome: How do I educate her?

Director: You teach her to appreciate wealth, power, and fame.

Handsome: How do I do that?

Director: Can't you guess?

Handsome: I suppose I can show her that we can use these things — for us.

Director: Very good. It's all for us. And I can see how you might use wealth. But how would you use power?

Handsome: Well, I'm not sure.

Director: That's alright. But what about fame?

Handsome: I'm not sure how we'd use fame, either.

Director: Maybe you could do without the fame? Retire into heavenly obscurity with your mate?

Handsome: That does sound awfully good.

Director: So as long as she isn't craving fame, there should be no reason why you can't do this. Right?

Handsome: I think that's true. But we'd still have the problem of not knowing how we'd use my power.

Director: Can't you get rid of your power just like you got rid of your fame?

Handsome: I don't know about that.

Director: Why not?

Handsome: Because... I... enjoy it too much.

50. POWER

Director: Well, let's think this through. If someone loves you, would she want you not to enjoy something that you truly enjoy?

Handsome: Of course not.

Director: But you don't just want to enjoy it, you want to enjoy it with her.

Handsome: Right.

Director: How would you do that? Would you share the power?

Handsome: I'm not sure that would be possible.

Director: Why not?

Handsome: Because it's... my power.

Director: Hmm. What about this? What if she enjoys seeing you enjoy your power, even though she wants nothing to do with it herself? Would that be good?

Handsome: She really enjoys it?

Director: Yes. And maybe in more ways than one. After all, haven't you heard that power is a great aphrodisiac?

Handsome: I have heard that.

Director: I suspect you've more than heard it, Handsome. So do we have it all settled now? You need someone who enjoys sharing wealth with you, enjoys your exercise of power, and enjoys a life far from fame.

Handsome: But I think there's a problem.

Director: Oh?

Handsome: Wealth and power typically bring fame.

Director: Do they? Then you'll just have to learn to be atypical.

51. Fame

Handsome: But the more I think about it, the less I like the idea of not having fame.

Director: Why?

Handsome: Because wealth and power without fame just seems wrong. So let's say I'm willing to be famous, at least among certain circles.

Director: So you'd have to find a mate who's not averse to limited fame.

Handsome: Right. We'd be famous, among those who know, together.

Director: And would you both enjoy your fame?

Handsome: That's the idea.

Director: And is the idea that shared fame would make you love one another more deeply?

Handsome: Enjoying things together makes for deeper love, yes.

Director: But there are pressures that come with fame, however limited — no?

Handsome: There are.

Director: Is it harder to deal with pressures alone or with someone else?

Handsome: The right someone else makes it easier.

Director: What makes someone the right someone else?

Handsome: Well, she loves me.

Director: Yes. But what characteristics does she have that make her deal well with pressure?

Handsome: That's a big question.

Director: How so?

Handsome: Those characteristics make up a large part of who she is.

Director: So fame in large part tests who you are?

Handsome: Yes, I think that's true.

Director: Then before fame, it's best if there's knowledge.

Handsome: I don't understand.

Director: To the degree fame tests who you are, it can make clear who you are.

Handsome: That's true.

Director: Well, if you don't know who you are and then you become famous, what happens?

Handsome: You might be in for a rude awakening.

Director: And if fame makes clear who your mate is, and you didn't know this before?

Handsome: You're either pleasantly, or unpleasantly, surprised.

52. Summing It Up

Director: So let's sum it up. You're looking for someone who comes to appreciate money, who enjoys your having power, and who likes the idea of and seems well disposed for fame.

Handsome: Yes, but those aren't the most important things.

Director: What are the most important things?

Handsome: Well, maybe it's only one thing. She has to love me — for me.

Director: You mean she has to love you for your physical you?

Handsome: No. For me! I'm more than my physical me.

Director: She has to love you for your heart, your mind, and your soul?

Handsome: Yes.

Director: Which of those is most important?

Handsome: The soul.

Director: What sort of soul have you got?

Handsome: What do you mean?

Director: I mean, are you what they call an old soul?

Handsome: No, I don't think I'm that.

Director: Then are you a young soul?

Handsome: Yes, I think I am.

Director: But how else can we describe your soul?

Handsome: It's really just a question of how you'd describe me. I am my soul.

Director: So your soul is good looking, rich, fairly powerful, and somewhat famous?

Handsome: You're teasing me.

Director: Alright. I'll say you're thoughtful, kind, curious — can you think of anything else?

Handsome: First of all, thank you. And can I think of anything else? It's not good to describe yourself.

Director: Modest — yes, you're modest, too. I think we've got a good start. The soul sums everything up, doesn't it?

Handsome: Yes, I think it does.

Director: The soul is everything about you — everything that counts.

Handsome: Yes.

Director: And, just to be sure — you want someone to love you for your soul.

Handsome: I do.

53. Love Me For Me

Director: But there's a problem with that.

Handsome: What problem?

Director: Are we perfect beings?

Handsome: Of course not.

Director: We have flaws?

Handsome: Yes.

Director: And our flaws are part of what makes up everything about us?

Handsome: True.

Director: Are we sure our souls are everything about us?

Handsome: Pretty sure.

Director: And if someone loves us for our soul, they love the flaws that our soul contains?

Handsome: People say that. But I'm not sure anyone actually loves a flaw. I mean, then it's not a flaw, right?

Director: That's what I'm inclined to think. But then what does this mean? Could it mean that your mate doesn't love you for your soul?

Handsome: What would your mate love you for, then?

Director: Your Me.

Handsome: Your Me is different than your soul?

Director: What do you think?

Handsome: I think that sounds a little crazy, Director.

Director: What would make it less crazy?

Handsome: Well, let's see. Are we saying Me is just the good parts of me?

Director: Yes, we are.

Handsome: And you want to be loved for the good parts of you?

Director: I do. Don't you?

Handsome: Yes. Then I guess we say — love me for Me.

54. PROFOUNDLY UN-PROFOUND

Director: Now, are we saying anything profound?

Handsome: No, I don't think so.

Director: But here's the thing. Love can be profound. Right?

Handsome: Of course.

Director: But Me, is Me profound?

Handsome: I think it can be. It just depends on the person.

Director: If your Me is given to love, and not the fleeting sort of love, but a deep, rich love — does that make your Me profound?

Handsome: Very.

Director: A profound Me needs a profound mate. Do you agree?

Handsome: Wholeheartedly.

Director: And a shallow Me needs a shallow mate?

Handsome: Yes.

Director: Is it good to be profound?

Handsome: Of course. It's very good.

Director: Is it good to be shallow?

Handsome: Honestly? I don't think it is.

Director: But we're still of the opinion that you love the good things in the other? And these good things are found in the Me. So you love the other's Me?

Handsome: That's right.

Director: Well, if it isn't good to be shallow, can shallowness ever be part of someone's Me?

Handsome: No, you have a point. It can't.

Director: So shallow people must find other things to love in their mates.

Handsome: I don't know, Director. I'm not sure shallow people actually love.

Director: Then what do they do?

Handsome: They fake.

55. FAKING

Director: Why would anyone ever want to fake love?

Handsome: Because they hear it's a good thing to have.

Director: But does this mean they've never felt love?

Handsome: I'm not sure. If they have felt love, they'll know they're faking. But if they've never felt love? How would they know their love is a fake?

Director: Which is worse? Having felt it or not having felt it?

Handsome: Again, I'm not sure. It's terrible to know you're faking. But it's also terrible never to have experienced love.

Director: What does it take to experience love?

Handsome: What do you mean?

Director: I mean, is it love if you feel you love someone but that person doesn't love you in turn?

Handsome: Oh, I see. No, that's not love. True love is only for those who reciprocate each other's love.

Director: Then what do people experience when they think they feel love for someone who doesn't reciprocate their love?

Handsome: I think it's probably best to call it infatuation or something like that.

Director: Is infatuation a deep or a shallow feeling?

Handsome: I guess we have to say it can be deep.

Director: Hmm.

Handsome: What's the matter?

Director: I'm wondering. Can two people be deeply infatuated with one another, reciprocally?

Handsome: You mean in a way that's not love?

Director: Yes.

Handsome: I suppose that's possible.

Director: Then how do we differentiate such infatuation from love?

56. INFATUATION

Handsome: Infatuation is blind.

Director: You mean the infatuated don't know the other for what he or she is?

Handsome: Exactly.

Director: But they think they see?

Handsome: Yes, but it's just an illusion.

Director: What brings on the illusion?

Handsome: I think it's usually got to do with circumstances.

Director: The stars have aligned?

Handsome: Yes.

Director: But what about love? Don't they say love is blind?

Handsome: They do. But they're talking about overlooking the physical defects a partner might have while focusing on the character, and so on.

Director: I thought it was about overlooking character defects, and so on. But, regardless, you're saying love isn't blind? Love sees?

Handsome: Love sees the Me.

Director: And when two people see each other's Me, in all its fullness, and they appreciate it, that's what it takes for love?

Handsome: That's what it takes.

Director: But getting back to the blind, when the stars fall out of alignment does the infatuation stop?

Handsome: Yes, almost always — but it can be very messy.

Director: Because one or both don't realize the stars have changed?

Handsome: Right.

Director: But once they do realize this they have a choice. They can spend their lives looking and hoping for the stars to align again, or they can set out and try to find their one true love.

Handsome: Unfortunately, I think most people spend their lives wishing on the stars.

Director: But let's make sure we're not being a little too harsh to the wrong people.

Handsome: How are we being too harsh and to whom?

Director: How easy do you think it is to find your true mate, the One who loves you?

Handsome: Not very easy at all.

Director: And if you've been looking for your love for a good long while both high and low, shouldn't we forgive you for looking up to the heavens every now and then and making a wish?

Handsome: You're right, of course. We certainly can forgive that. It's fine to hope for love. But only fools hope to find infatuation again.

57. FLEETING LOVE, 2

Director: Tell me, Handsome. Aren't those who long for infatuation the ones people refer to as being addicted to love?

Handsome: Yes, I think you're right. But they're really addicted to infatuation.

Director: And what about what we've been calling fleeting love? Is that really just a case of infatuation? Or is it a sort of love?

Handsome: I don't know. What do you think?

Director: Maybe it's a little of both.

Handsome: How so?

Director: Maybe there's an alignment of the stars, the circumstances that make for infatuation. And maybe there's also a true appreciation of some of the Me.

Handsome: But not all of the Me?

Director: Right. What do you think?

Handsome: It's infatuation, not love.

Director: Why?

Handsome: Director, didn't we just say that love, real love, sees all of the Me, and appreciates it?

Director: We did.

Handsome: Then if fleeting love only sees part of the Me, we know it isn't love.

58. APPRECIATING

Director: There's a pleasure in seeing even only a part of someone's Me, isn't there?

Handsome: Yes, of course. It's always nice to find something worth appreciating in another. But that doesn't mean you're in love.

Director: Yes. But here's something I'm wondering. If you were starved for appreciation, and someone appreciated a part of you, someone you were attracted to — might you think it was love?

Handsome: Yes, that happens. And it's very sad. I think the under-appreciated one is simply overwhelmed.

Director: Then is it the duty of the one who appreciates to make clear how things stand?

Handsome: Absolutely.

Director: I imagine a person with your gifts would have to do this often, if he's in the business of appreciating people.

Handsome: Yes, it's true.

Director: And does it ever happen that the making things clear overshadows the appreciation?

Handsome: You've put your finger precisely on the problem. That does happen from time to time. And it's almost enough to make you not want to appreciate people anymore.

Director: What makes you want to appreciate people?

Handsome: I think it's just a good, simple, human desire to recognize the good in others.

Director: If that's true, then why doesn't everyone do it?

Handsome: Because, simply — not everyone is good.

Director: If you're not good, is it that you don't see the good in others or is it that you see it and don't want to recognize it?

Handsome: I think you see it and don't want to recognize it.

Director: Why would you not want to recognize it?

Handsome: Because the good bothers the bad. It irritates them.

Director: Does that mean the bad can never truly love the good?

Handsome: The bad can never love anything at all.

59. Good, Better, Happy

Director: Why can't the bad love?

Handsome: Because if they loved, they'd be good!

Director: Love makes us good?

Handsome: Yes, of course.

Director: So we can be sure that someone devoid of love is bad?

Handsome: Positively sure.

Director: Then that means those who only know infatuation are bad?

Handsome: Well, I'm not sure I'd say they're simply bad. They can have good qualities.

Director: What good qualities can they have? Love makes us good. They don't know love. They only know infatuation.

Handsome: Yes, but that's just romantic love.

Director: Ah, I see. Non-romantic love can make us good, too.

Handsome: Of course.

Director: And you can be infatuated and still have non-romantic love.

Handsome: Right.

Director: But you'd be better if you had both non-romantic and true romantic love?

Handsome: No doubt.

Director: But how do you know?

Handsome: What do you mean?

Director: I mean, you haven't found that sort of romantic love, have you? So how do you know it would make you better?

Handsome: I know because I've seen it happen to others.

Director: Friends who were good became better when they found their love?

Handsome: Yes, without a doubt.

Director: They became better toward you?

Handsome: Of course. Why do you ask?

Director: Because they might have become better, then retreated into their paradise of love, leaving you behind.

Handsome: Well, it's true I don't see them as often I used to.

Director: Because you've yet to become better yourself and aren't allowed to enter the gates of paradise?

Handsome: Tease me all you want. I know they've become better regardless of how much time I spend with them.

Director: But if you don't spend much time with them....

Handsome: Then how do I know? It's easy, Director. When I see them it's as clear as day. They're happy.

60. FULFILLMENT

Director: Do you think that being better makes us happy or is it that being happy makes us better?

Handsome: I don't think it works like that.

Director: Why not?

Handsome: Because love makes us both better and happy at the same time

Director: Is there anything else like love, anything that can make us both better and happy at once?

Handsome: Not that I can think of.

Director: But if we found something like that, would we have found that we don't need love?

Handsome: Of course not.

Director: Why?

Handsome: Because even if we find something that makes us better and happy, a sort of substitute for love, we would lack one thing.

Director: What?

Handsome: Fulfillment.

Director: You can't be fulfilled without love?

Handsome: That's right.

Director: Does it have to be a particular type of love?

Handsome: Yes, romantic love.

Director: Really? You can't feel fulfilled through the love of friends?

Handsome: It's not the same.

Director: Hmm. What about feeling fulfilled through doing something you truly love doing?

Handsome: You mean if I love my work I'll feel fulfilled?

Director: Yes.

Handsome: That's definitely not the same.

Director: But surely you think there's at least some fulfillment that comes from friends, or family, or an activity you love.

Handsome: Well, of course. So let's just say you can feel some fulfillment without romantic love, but not as much as you would with it.

Director: But you know what we're saying, don't you?

Handsome: What?

Director: We're saying fulfillment admits of degree.

Handsome: But, Director, don't you know? Everything admits of degree.

61. BETTER AND HAPPY

Director: I'm not sure that's true. But let's get back to being better and happy. What does it mean to be better and happy? What goes into being better and happy?

Handsome: I don't see why it matters. If we're better, we're better. If we're happy, we're happy. And that's that.

Director: But are we just going to hold out for love to make us better and happy to the highest degree? Or is it worth our while to find another way, a temporary way — a way we can rely on until we find our One?

Handsome: Well, it's as you said. We have other sorts of love.

Director: And one of those is the love of something we do. That can make us better, can't it?

Handsome: How?

Director: How? Look at it this way. If I love running, and I train hard and come to run faster than before — what am I?

Handsome: You're a better runner.

Director: And if I love cooking, and I learn how to make a dish much more wonderful than any I had made before — what am I?

Handsome: You're a better chef.

Director: In both cases I'm better at something specific, right?

Handsome: Right.

Director: And it would make me happy to be better at these things?

Handsome: Let's say it would, to a certain degree.

Director: And only to a certain degree because this is no substitute for romantic love?

Handsome: Yes.

Director: Well then, let's consider romantic love. Can we be better at this?

Handsome: Better at love?

Director: Yes. Can we?

Handsome: I have a problem with this.

Director: Because you don't think it's possible?

Handsome: Here's the thing, Director. Love isn't an activity like running or cooking. It just... is!

Director: Ah, well that's where you're wrong.

62. LOVE

Handsome: How is love an activity?

Director: What do you do when you're in love?

Handsome: What do you mean?

Director: Do you just stare into each other's eyes all day long?

Handsome: No, of course not.

Director: So when you're not staring into each other's eyes, what do you do?

Handsome: We just... do things!

Director: What sort of things?

Handsome: It could be anything.

Director: But the point is that you're doing these things together?

Handsome: Right.

Director: And doing these things with your love is better than doing these things on your own?

Handsome: Very much so.

Director: Is that because you're interacting with your love while you do these things, or is there some other reason?

Handsome: It's because we're interacting.

Director: Well, so far so good.

Handsome: Yes, but just because you interact with your love doesn't mean that love itself is an activity.

Director: Then tell me. Do you think we're born knowing all we need to know about love, or do you think we can learn something about it?

Handsome: I suppose we can learn something about it.

Director: And if we can learn, we can become better?

Handsome: I suppose I have to admit that's true.

Director: Now, when it comes to being better, what makes more sense? Being better at something we can't do, or being better at something we can do?

Handsome: Something we can do.

Director: And when we get better at love, what exactly can we do?

Handsome: I don't know.

Director: You really don't know?

Handsome: We can interact better with our mate.

Director: Is interacting an activity?

Handsome: Yes, but it's a very general sort of activity.

Director: Not like running faster? Not like cooking a new dish?

Handsome: Exactly.

Director: What do you think is more difficult? Learning how to interact better with your mate, or learning how to cook or run?

Handsome: If I'm honest? Learning how to interact with my mate.

Director: And do you think that running faster and cooking new dishes are more important than interacting with your mate?

Handsome: Of course not.

Director: So interacting with your mate is both more difficult and more important than cooking and running. Does that somehow make it less of an activity than those things?

Handsome: No.

Director: Does it make it at least every bit as much an activity?

Handsome: I feel compelled to say yes. But I'm not sure about our reasoning. And I have an objection. What about when lovers are together and simply do nothing? That's not really an activity. They just enjoy each other's company.

Director: Here's how it seems to me. What you're talking about feels good because of activities you've already performed. Or do you think you'd feel good just being with someone you haven't interacted with at all? No, it's the prior activity of love, of interacting with your mate, that makes doing nothing so sweet.

Handsome: I guess that's true. But there's one last objection. If love is an activity, why do we refer to it as a state — as being in love?

63. IN LOVE

Director: People talk about 'being in love' because of a great confusion.

Handsome: What confusion?

Director: The confusion caused by the infatuated. They're the ones who started all of this kind of talk.

Handsome: And people just followed their lead?

Director: Yes, those who didn't know love. And you can imagine how many there were.

Handsome: So why do the infatuated talk about being in love?

Director: It comes naturally to them because they don't truly interact with each other.

Handsome: Why not?

Director: Because of their illusions, their dreams. You see, when they 'interact' it's with an illusory, dreamlike idea of what the other is as opposed to what the other truly is.

Handsome: But what about true lovers? Are they dreaming?

Director: No, they're very much awake. And they truly interact with their love.

Handsome: But what if the infatuated wake up? Isn't it possible that some of them might find themselves with their loves, their true loves?

Director: Yes, I think it's possible. And imagine the scene when they first try interacting as lovers! Comedy.

Handsome: Yes, and that's good! We don't exactly want tragedy.

Director: Right. So is that enough about 'being in love'?

Handsome: I'm satisfied. But I'm still going to talk about love as a state!

64. TRAGIC

Director: I won't dare try to stop you. But tell me. We mentioned tragedy and comedy. Do you think all good, healthy love is more comic than not?

Handsome: More comic than tragic? Yes, of course.

Director: And that's so even if the lovers are surrounded by tragic circumstances?

Handsome: Well, that would make comic interaction hard.

Director: What makes for comic interaction?

Handsome: Keeping your spirits up. Keeping things light rather than heavy. And so on.

Director: And that's all much easier when circumstances tilt toward the comic?

Handsome: Of course.

Director: So what should we think of lovers who give themselves to tragic interaction when comic conditions prevail?

Handsome: But why would they do that?

Director: Do you know what many people would say?

Handsome: No, what?

Director: That some people like to feel sorry for themselves.

Handsome: So they imagine there are tragic circumstances where none exist?

Director: What do you think?

Handsome: I think it's true. So we need to make a distinction.

Director: Between what?

Handsome: True tragic circumstances and those that exist only in the mind.

Director: What's a true tragic circumstance?

Handsome: War, or famine, or terribly hostile and abusive environments, and all else you can imagine along those lines.

Director: I see. So let's suppose none of these true tragic circumstances exist. And let's suppose a lover comes along and sees her love given to tragedy in the mind. What should she do?

Handsome: Help pull her love free.

Director: How strong do you think she'd have to be to help pull her love free?

Handsome: Very.

Director: And what do you think this very strong lover would get out of it?

Handsome: Get out of it? Why, love, Director!

Director: Yes, of course. But I was wondering if there might be something else.

Handsome: What else?

Director: Knowledge of the tragedy of the mind, perhaps?

Handsome: Yes, I suppose you have a point.

Director: But she has to be careful, Handsome. This sort of tragedy can be seductive.

Handsome: So what can she do?

Director: She'll have to bring a comic sensibility to her study of the tragic.

Handsome: Yes, and maybe she could learn to do the opposite.

Director: What do you mean?

Handsome: She could learn to bring a tragic sensibility to the study of the comic.

Director: Now you're treading dangerous ground, my friend.

Handsome: Why?

Director: If you color the bright hue of the comic black, there's no guarantee it will ever wash clean.

Handsome: Okay. But if you had to say in a word what it takes to cure a tragic soul, to help pull it free, what would it be?

Director: Love. And not a flat and heavy love. But a light and sparkling love.

65. LIGHT AND SPARKLING

Handsome: You mean like champagne?

Director: Yes.

Handsome: Well, how can lovers keep their love like that?

Director: Let's consider the opposite and maybe we'll see. What do you think that is?

Handsome: The opposite of champagne? Let's say it's oil.

Director: Okay. What's the closest we can come to making oil like champagne?

Handsome: I have no idea. What do you think?

Director: We can burn it.

Handsome: Burning oil is like champagne? That sounds crazy.

Director: Well, can you think of any other way to make the two alike?

Handsome: No, none at all. Oil is oil and champagne is champagne.

Director: So how do the tragic and the comic figure into this?

Handsome: I suppose the tragic will tend toward the oil flame and the comic will tend toward the sparkle of the light wine. And if they become lovers, they might play a sort of game.

Director: A game? How so?

Handsome: They might go back and forth — flame to sparkle, and sparkle to flame.

Director: I don't know, Handsome. Do you really think someone tragically inclined will be good at a game like that? It seems to me that a comic soul can go to a flame and appreciate it. But a tragic soul can go to a sparkle — and not appreciate it one little bit. Do you think I'm getting at something essential about tragedy and comedy, or am I just making this up?

Handsome: No, I think there's truth to what you say. So comedy always wins.

Director: But isn't there a greater victory to be had?

Handsome: I suppose the ultimate victory would be to get tragedy to appreciate the sparkle. But how can comedy do that?

Director: Can't you imagine, Handsome? Comedy must get tragedy to drink the champagne. And if tragedy develops a taste for it? Well, then both comedy and tragedy have won.

66. The Game

Handsome: But what happens if comedy comes to love the game?

Director: What do you mean?

Handsome: I mean, what if once they win, and tragedy learns to enjoy the champagne of love, comedy feels compelled to go on to play somewhere else, with someone else who needs its help. Wouldn't that be awful?

Director: Why, exactly?

Handsome: The point is to be lovers, happily ever after!

Director: But don't you think comedy helped?

Handsome: But all the wine is going to evaporate once comedy is gone!

Director: So the tragic lover is going to fall away from the sparkle in life?

Handsome: Almost certainly.

Director: Unless tragedy can become comic itself.

Handsome: How likely do you think that is?

Director: Well, hasn't it had some coaching? Now it just needs to do it on its own.

Handsome: I just can't get over how terrible this is.

Director: Because you think comedy loved the game and didn't love tragedy?

Handsome: Yes.

Director: I disagree. I do think comedy loved tragedy.

Handsome: Just not with the love of a One?

Director: Yes. And look at the good that came of it. Tragedy's eyes are wide open now, looking out for its true comic One.

Handsome: But now it's my turn to disagree. I think tragedy wants a tragic lover now.

Director: A tragic lover? Why?

Handsome: So it can take up the role of comic lover itself, as you've suggested — and win a great victory with its one and only tragic One.

67. A Problem

Director: I see. But tell me. What tends to be deeper in soul — the tragic or the comic?

Handsome: I'd have to say the tragic.

Director: If that's true, then what stops tragedy-made-comedy from sinking back down into its old tragic depths as it tries to pull its newly found tragic love up from the deep?

Handsome: Why, all that it learned while with comedy.

Director: I hope it learned to tell if someone is playing a game.

Handsome: What game?

Director: The game its tragic lover might play.

Handsome: What kind of game could it play?

Director: The game that brings you down.

Handsome: You mean a tragic lover will try to pull a comic lover into the deep?

Director: Of course.

Handsome: But now I'm getting confused.

Director: How so?

Handsome: Love is profound. And the profound is the deep. So what's wrong with a tragic lover pulling a comic lover into the deep, the deep of love?

Director: Yes, you've put your finger on a problem.

Handsome: That's all you can say?

Director: What do you want me to say?

Handsome: That the deep is good.

Director: If I say that, I'm going to say that the comic is just as deep as the tragic.

Handsome: We can say that.

Director: And if we say that deep is good and that the comic is deep, you know what else I'm going to say?

Handsome: Tell me.

Director: I'm going to say that the comic is not only deep but is also clear.

Handsome: Is the tragic clear?

Director: I have to say no. The tragic needs the comic in order to clear itself up.

Handsome: But then doesn't the tragic simply become the comic? After all, they would both be deep and clear.

Director: Then maybe we have to take a drastic step.

Handsome: What step?

Director: We have to say that when things are deep and clear on both sides, there's no such thing as tragic or comic — there's only love. What do you think?

Handsome: I think it makes sense.

Director: That's good, because as for me — I'm not so sure.

68. DEEP AND CLEAR

Handsome: But what aren't you sure about? Don't you think deep and clear love is the ideal?

Director: I think it's an ideal. But I'm not sure it can ever be reached.

Handsome: But that's what ideals are for! You don't have to reach them. You just have to be guided by them.

Director: So are we saying to all lovers, young and old — go deep, and stay clear?

Handsome: Yes, and what's wrong with that?

Director: Tell me, Handsome. Do you think most people are deep, or are most people shallow?

Handsome: Truthfully? I think most people are shallow.

Director: If we tell shallow people to go deep, what happens?

Handsome: Nothing.

Director: And now tell me. Do you think most people have water that's clear, or is it muddied?

Handsome: What I really think? I think most people have muddy waters inside.

Director: What happens if we tell the muddy to stay clear?

Handsome: Again, I'd say, nothing.

Director: So if we tell everyone, go deep and stay clear, for the most part nothing will happen. But for some?

Handsome: For some this will be an inspiration.

Director: And it's worth inspiring them?

Handsome: Very much so.

Director: Why?

Handsome: Because they'll improve the quality of their love! And there's something else.

Director: What else?

Handsome: When they're inspired they'll feel good about themselves — and when they feel good they're more likely to make friends.

69. FRIENDS AND LOVERS

Director: Do you think that's the only true friendship? The deep and clear with the deep and clear?

Handsome: Don't you?

Director: Let's say it's the ideal. But what about your One?

Handsome: Your One is the only one who can see all the way down to the bottom in you.

Director: Not even your best of friends can see all the way down?

Handsome: If he or she can, where does that leave your One?

Director: In good company.

Handsome: But The One wants to be unique.

Director: Well, maybe she is.

Handsome: How so?

Director: Maybe she's the only one who will actually dive in and touch bottom.

Handsome: Ah, I think that's an excellent point.

Director: And that's the difference between lovers and friends?

Handsome: That's the difference.

Director: But both will appreciate the sight of sparkling clear water and depth?

Handsome: Very much so.

Director: But only the lover will know, truly know, what's on bottom — whether it's fine, clean, and beautiful sand; or whether it's mud and muck.

Handsome: I'm not sure about that.

Director: Oh?

Handsome: You're not accounting for storms.

Director: Storms? What do you mean?

Handsome: Imagine a storm powerful enough to bring up what's on bottom. Can you imagine that?

Director: I can.

Handsome: Well, if a great emotional storm stirs our friend, what's at bottom is bound to come up — for all of us to see.

70. At Bottom

Director: And when our friend calms back down, whatever came up from the bottom will eventually settle back down and we'll see his clear water again?

Handsome: Yes. What do you think?

Director: I think that makes a good deal of sense. But what about someone who never has storms?

Handsome: Never? I don't believe it. Everyone has storms from time to time.

Director: What about those who can feel a storm coming and go off by themselves to ride it out?

Handsome: If they always do that? Then I suppose we'll never know what they're made of at bottom.

Director: And so what if we don't? If someone is good clear water to our souls, do we really care?

Handsome: If the water is really good and clear? I guess we don't. But lovers still care. They want to get to the bottom of things — even if that bottom isn't perfect sand.

Director: Lovers want to know.

Handsome: Yes.

Director: But if when they get to the bottom they feel clean sand — what's to know?

Handsome: But that's what they wanted to know!

Director: Okay. But what if they find some muck?

Handsome: What do you mean by 'muck'?

Director: Half-digested experiences, lies to the self.

Handsome: Well, here's the thing. If the love is true, your lover understands you're not perfect. If not, the two of you weren't meant to be.

71. MUCK

Director: But if your lover does understand, what do you think the next step is?

Handsome: Being patient with you as you try to clean up your muck. And maybe something more.

Director: What more?

Handsome: Maybe your lover can help you with the muck.

Director: How do you think he or she will do that?

Handsome: Don't get me wrong. I think this is a job that, essentially, you have to do on your own. I mean, who's going to digest your half-digested experiences but you? But maybe there's something your lover can do concerning the lies you tell yourself.

Director: Tell you the truth about them?

Handsome: Yes. What do you think?

Director: I think that's no easy thing to ask of someone. It takes some powerful love to speak truth to a soul in the habit of telling even a single lie to itself.

Handsome I agree. It takes a One. But we should remember that each time after dealing with the muck, your lover can swim back up to the beautiful, sparkling water above.

Director: And you don't think that sounds a little too good to be true?

Handsome: You think the telling of the truth will stir up the muck, will muddy the waters?

Director: Do you?

Handsome: Well, yes. But sometimes that's what it takes to make things clear.

Director: It's always darkest before the dawn?

Handsome: Exactly.

Director: And when the dawn comes, and shines upon our waters — what will it reveal?

Handsome: Sparkling clarity.

Director: And when the lover dives in?

Handsome: There will be that much less muck, and that much more clean and beautiful sand.

72. GROUND

Director: At this point I think it makes sense to alter the metaphor.

Handsome: How so?

Director: Instead of sand, let's talk about ground.

Handsome: Why?

Director: Because then we can talk about standing our ground.

Handsome: And if we reclaim our ground from lies to the self and half digested experiences, we'll be better able to stand?

Director: Yes. So tell me. Would you like to find a mate who stands her ground?

Handsome: Of course I would.

Director: But if you're standing your ground and she's standing hers — what common ground do you have?

Handsome: Director, don't you know? Her ground and my ground are the same.

Director: And that's one way in which two lovers are one?

Handsome: Yes.

Director: Well, that's good. But let me ask you this. What is your ground?

Handsome: Well-digested experiences and truths instead of lies.

Director: And you share your experiences and truths with your love?

Handsome: Yes, of course.

Director: Are there others with whom you share these things?

Handsome: I share them with my friends.

Director: But do you share your ground as perfectly with them as with your love?

Handsome: Well, no.

Director: But if there were one of them with whom you could?

Handsome: Then I'd be a very lucky man.

73. CIRCLES

Director: Yes. But we can still have a good circle of friends despite imperfectly shared ground, right?

Handsome: We certainly can.

Director: Now here's what I'm wondering. If we have a circle, do we want it be very small or do we want it to be as large as possible?

Handsome: Well, that's an interesting question.

Director: Why?

Handsome: Because on the one hand there's something wonderfully intimate about a small circle.

Director: But on the other hand?

Handsome: Our circle shares experiences and truths, right?

Director: Right.

Handsome: Well, when you combine those things you get knowledge. And don't we want to share our knowledge as broadly as we can?

Director: A good point. But will all those we share knowledge with necessarily join our circle?

Handsome: Why wouldn't they?

Director: Well, for one they might not share the underlying experience.

Handsome: Ah, I see what you mean. So no, they don't all join our circle.

Director: Then does that mean it might be possible to both share our knowledge and keep our circle small?

Handsome: Yes, I think it does.

Director: So what will it be?

Handsome: We'll keep our circle small.

Director: Now, in our small circle, can you guess what might happen?

Handsome: No, what?

Director: Aside from the original pairs, such as you and your love, might not more loving pairs come to form?

Handsome: That's true. But I'm not sure I like that.

Director: Why not?

Handsome: Because it seems a bit... incestuous.

Director: So what can we do?

Handsome: Find lovers on the outside and bring them in.

Director: But doesn't that grow the circle?

Handsome: Yes, but it's better to grow given the alternative.

Director: What good comes of growth?

Handsome: There will be an infusion of fresh ideas.

Director: But I thought common ground is the thing.

Handsome: It can't be the only thing.

Director: So what do these fresh ideas do?

Handsome: They add life to the circle.

Director: What happens when you add life to a circle?

Handsome: It grows. And not just in numbers, but in experiences and truths.

Director: And if new ideas keep coming in?

Handsome: The circle keeps growing.

Director: Yes, but I wonder if you've heard about this.

Handsome: What?

Director: Certain circles, when they grow to a certain size, divide. And then there are two smaller, similar circles.

Handsome: I have heard about that.

Director: Do you think it's a good thing for that to happen?

Handsome: I think it can be.

Director: Why?

Handsome: Because it makes things diverse. These smaller circles still share common ground. But they develop in different ways.

Director: And eventually they, too, might divide?

Handsome: Yes, and so on, and so on. In the end, we come to have a world filled with circles.

Director: But don't we have that now?

Handsome: Yes. But with one important difference.

Director: What?

Handsome: Not all of our circles have love.

74. Bad Circles

Director: Are you saying it's possible to belong to a circle and not feel any love, not only romantically speaking, but also in the sense of the love of friends?

Handsome: Of course it's possible.

Director: Why would anyone ever belong to such a circle?

Handsome: Because they feel trapped.

Director: What traps them?

Handsome: It's hard to explain.

Director: Give it a try.

Handsome: They... just don't... know any better.

Director: How could they come to know better?

Handsome: I suppose they could visit our circle.

Director: And if they want to join?

Handsome: Well, that's the hard part. They can't.

Director: Why not?

Handsome: Because they don't share enough common ground.

Director: But how are they any different than lovers brought in from outside?

Handsome: The outside lovers share common ground with their inside lovers before they come in.

Director: Hmm. Maybe there's nothing we can do. Unless....

Handsome: Unless?

Director: Unless we send ambassadors to the bad circles.

Handsome: Why would we want to do that?

Director: Why, to teach those who want to know about our ground. And then to invite those who prove they can stand that ground to join us. What do you think?

75. Ambassadors

Handsome: I don't know. Who's going to be willing to leave our circle to go to theirs?

Director: Someone who wants to learn.

Handsome: But what is there to learn?

Director: What those capable of joining our circle can teach. Or don't you think we can learn anything from them?

Handsome: No, of course we can. But what if we want to learn like this, but we have mates who don't want to leave home?

Director: You're asking what happens to our relationships if we leave our mates behind?

Handsome: Yes.

Director: Is it the absence that worries you most?

Handsome: No, a healthy love can deal with that.

Director: Then what?

Handsome: We might change.

Director: How so?

Handsome: We might learn things that change us.

Director: And if we're going to keep our relationships with our mates intact?

Handsome: We'll have to teach our mates what we know.

Director: And what about our friends?

Handsome: We'll have to teach them, too.

Director: And they'll have to teach their friends and mates, and so on, until, eventually, the whole circle comes to know?

Handsome: Yes.

Director: Is the circle stronger or weaker for knowing?

Handsome: Stronger, of course. We're always stronger when we know.

Director: If that's true, then can you see how important ambassadors can be?

Handsome: I can.

76. Together

Director: So what happens if two lovers serve together as ambassadors?

Handsome: Well, I would worry about that.

Director: Why?

Handsome: Because the job is so demanding.

Director: And that might cause strain?

Handsome: Yes.

Director: What's the hardest part of the job?

Handsome: Both the teaching and the learning.

Director: But if our couple loves both teaching and learning?

Handsome: Then there might be hope.

Director: Why?

Handsome: Because doing something you love, together, can strengthen a relationship.

Director: I think that's true. But what about teaching and learning is difficult?

Handsome: The resistance.

Director: The resistance?

Handsome: The others might resist what they can learn from us. And we might resist what we can learn from them.

Director: But if we love what we're doing?

Handsome: Then we don't mind their resistance as much. And we find ways of overcoming our own.

Director: When would we feel most satisfied? If we accomplished something against no resistance, or if we accomplished something against great resistance?

Handsome: If we accomplished it against great resistance.

Director: So if our ambassadors seek satisfaction?

Handsome: They'll go to where the work is difficult.

Director: And how will they know when it's time to move on?

Handsome: They'll know when things have gotten too easy.

Director: What got too easy? The teaching or the learning?

Handsome: Both.

77. TEACHING AND LEARNING

Director: When we teach and learn, do we want to teach and learn just any difficult thing, or do we want to teach and learn something important?

Handsome: Something important.

Director: What's more important than love?

Handsome: Than love? Why, nothing.

Director: So our lovers go around teaching and learning about love?

Handsome: You're trying to make it sound ridiculous.

Director: Am I? Then tell me something important that isn't love, something people want to teach, something people want to learn — something that's difficult to teach and learn.

Handsome: It's difficult to teach and learn about life.

Director: And what's the most important thing in life?

Handsome: Well, love.

Director: You see? There's no getting away from it.

Handsome: In that case our lovers better be sure to learn the same things about love at the same time.

Director: Why?

Handsome: Because they'll be out of sorts if they don't.

Director: Can you say more?

Handsome: Sure. Suppose one lover learns that love requires, for instance, patience — and the other one doesn't. Can't you see how that might be a problem?

Director: I don't know, Handsome. Let me tell you how it seems to me. Before one lover learned about patience, both lovers were impatient?

Handsome: Yes.

Director: And impatience puts strain on a relationship?

Handsome: True.

Director: So if one lover learns to be patient, won't there be that much less strain?

Handsome: I know what you're saying. But here's the thing. There will be a new strain.

Director: What sort of strain?

Handsome: The strain the one who learned patience will feel.

Director: Why will he or she feel strain?

Handsome: Because the patience isn't reciprocated.

Director: So it's not just love that should be reciprocated? It's patience, too?

Handsome: Yes.

Director: Would this be so with any of the qualities pertaining to love?

Handsome: I think so.

Director: So if only one partner learns about one of these qualities, whatever it might be, and puts it into practice, that party, and only that party, feels strain?

Handsome: Of course.

Director: Well, that's where we differ.

Handsome: How so?

Director: I'm inclined to think that, in the case of true love, when one party feels strain, both parties feel strain.

Handsome: Why?

Director: If you learned patience and your lover hadn't, how would you feel?

Handsome: As I said, strained — and annoyed.

Director: Don't you think your lover, your One, would notice your annoyance?

Handsome: Yes, I suppose — if she's truly my One.

Director: Right. I mean, what kind of lover wouldn't notice when you're annoyed?

Handsome: I take the point.

Director: And if you notice that someone as important as your lover is annoyed with you, how would you feel?

Handsome: You wouldn't feel good.

Director: Would you feel tense, feel a strain?

Handsome: Yes.

Director: So both sides feel the strain.

Handsome: True enough.

Director: What would lessen the strain?

Handsome: The impatient one learning patience.

Director: Or?

Handsome: I'm not sure what you have in mind.

Director: What can the patient one do?

Handsome: Become less patient?

Director: Yes, and why would he or she do that?

Handsome: Because too much patience means you're not speaking up about things that bother you.

Director: And what happens when you don't?

Handsome: You feel annoyed and strained.

Director: Are you really being patient if you're annoyed and strained? Is that what patience means?

Handsome: No, I don't think it does.

Director: So that means you have more to learn about patience — about how much is enough, but not too much. No?

Handsome: Yes, I suppose it that's true.

Director: And how will you know when you've got the right amount?

Handsome: If you're with your One? You'll know by the harmony in your love.

78. HARMONY

Director: What is harmony?

Handsome: You mean in musical terms?

Director: Yes.

Handsome: It's when you play notes together to produce a pleasing sound.

Director: Do you know what's striking about that definition?

Handsome: No, what?

Director: It's what you left out.

Handsome: What do you mean?

Director: You didn't mention that the notes you play are different notes.

Handsome: But of course they're different notes.

Director: Then why don't we talk about different notes when it comes to harmony in a love relationship?

Handsome: You mean if one note is patience, another might be... impatience?

Director: Do you think patience and impatience can harmonize?

Handsome: I don't know. Isn't there a word for a good form of impatience?

Director: Keenness.

Handsome: Yes. You can be patient and keen at once, can't you?

Director: Yes, I think you can. But I wonder what this means if your love is only one of these things but you're both.

Handsome: You mean I'm patient and keen but she's only keen?

Director: Yes.

Handsome: Well, her keenness would harmonize with my patience.

Director: Just as your keenness would harmonize with your patience?

Handsome: Yes, I guess that's true.

Director: So you harmonize with each other in part. And you harmonize with yourself. But your lover, she can't harmonize with herself. Can she?

Handsome: No, I don't think she can.

Director: But you'd like your love to harmonize with herself? Wouldn't you?

Handsome: Of course. I'd like her to have patience. Both for her own sake and so she can better harmonize with me.

Director: And doesn't this hold for all kinds of things?

Handsome: Like what?

Director: Well, let's take assertiveness. What can fill that out as a chord?

Handsome: Being laid back?

Director: Yes, I think it can. You can be assertive and laid back at once. And what about curiosity? What makes a chord with that?

Handsome: Being pleased to know what you already know?

Director: Yes, I think that can make for a chord. You're glad you know but want to know more.

Handsome: I like what we're saying. And when I'm looking for my One I'll be sure that she's in harmony with herself and with me.

79. Different Strings

Director: Now, I'm not trying to stir up trouble. But do you know the basic fact about chords, about harmonies?

Handsome: Tell me.

Director: The notes are either on different instruments, or on different strings on the same instrument. And, yes, I know this doesn't always hold. A pipe organ is an instrument that has no strings and yet it can create harmonies, chords. But you get the basic point?

Handsome: Yes, I get the point.

Director: Now, if you had the love of your life, would you, in harmonizing with her, want her to be a completely different instrument or just a different string on the same instrument as you?

Handsome: A different string.

Director: Why?

Handsome: Because then we'd be on the same instrument.

Director: You'd be closer that way.

Handsome: Yes. Precisely.

Director: So you'd limit yourself.

Handsome: What do you mean?

Director: Rather than be a full instrument, you'd settle to be part of an instrument.

Handsome: No. With my love I'd be a full instrument.

Director: A two stringed instrument?

Handsome: No, we could have more strings than that.

Director: You could be something like a guitar, with six strings?

Handsome: Sure, and that would make us whole.

Director: But tell me, Handsome. Would you only play on your three strings, or would you play on hers, too?

Handsome: Well, I'd have to learn her strings in order to do that. And she would have to learn mine.

Director: You wouldn't be opposed to that?

Handsome: Opposed to learning how to play each other's strings? I'd be a fool to be opposed to that.

Director: Why?

Handsome: Because that's how each of us becomes the whole instrument. And that's how beautiful music is made.

80. Closer

Director: So let me ask you this. You want closeness, yes?

Handsome: Of course.

Director: Well, what's closer than playing together on one and only one string?

Handsome: Nothing. But then only one note at a time can be played. And then there's no harmony.

Director: So harmony requires some distance, the distance between strings?

Handsome: Yes, absolutely.

Director: But what if your love can't see that? She can only see that you're not on the same string.

Handsome: And she has a problem with that? Then maybe she's not for me.

Director: Because harmony is more important than closeness?

Handsome: Look, closeness is important — so important. But what are we going to do? Just play the same note together all the time?

Director: Harmony is more beautiful than a single pure note?

Handsome: I'm not saying that. Pure notes can be beautiful.

Director: So you won't object to a single note from time to time?

Handsome: No, I won't object — as long as we continue to harmonize from time to time, too.

Director: Then tell me what you'd do if you're on your guitar, and you've been playing single notes with your love for a long while, and you feel her trying to climb onto one of your strings to play yet another single note with you.

Handsome: We'd have to have a talk.

Director: And if that doesn't work?

Handsome: I may seriously have to consider becoming my own instrument.

Director: No shared strings?

Handsome: No shared strings.

Director: And all because you're not getting enough harmony out of the relationship?

Handsome: Does that surprise you?

Director: Well, yes. Don't you think most people want unity?

Handsome: Yes. But they also want room to breathe.

Director: And harmony gives you that room, that air?

Handsome: Right.

Director: So, far from being a petty dispute over music, this is a matter, spiritually speaking, of life and death?

Handsome: I agree. And before I'd let this kill me I'd end the relationship.

Director: But what about going on but as separate instruments?

Handsome: Separate instruments can play the same note, too.

Director: Then if nothing works, that's it?

Handsome: That's it.

81. SILENCE

Director: Then is it safe to say that staying together requires mutual appreciation of music, of a certain type of music that's more than just single notes at a time?

Handsome: Yes.

Director: But what if you don't appreciate music?

Handsome: Any music?

Director: Yes, any music. What's the term? Amusical? What if you're amusical?

Handsome: You'd have a very hard time harmonizing with a lover, Director.

Director: So do you think it's best for such a person not to get into a relationship?

Handsome: But what if he or she is someone who deserves to have a relationship?

Director: Maybe he or she can find an amusical mate.

Handsome: But what would they do? Just make noise together?

Director: I suppose they could just keep quiet together.

Handsome: Well, there's that.

Director: What? Weren't you the one who said doing nothing together can be important? But surely you know there's an art to this, an art that some of the rarest of lovers practice?

Handsome: The art of silence?

Director: Yes.

Handsome: Why is silence better than music?

Director: For this couple? It's obvious, isn't it?

Handsome: Yes, but why is it better for everyone?

Director: Oh, I wouldn't say it's better for everyone.

Handsome: Music is best for some, and silence is best for others?

Director: I couldn't have said it better myself.

Handsome: But what do people get out of silence?

Director: What else, my friend — but peace?

82. PEACE

Handsome: But that should be what everyone gets out of a relationship.

Director: You mean music brings peace?

Handsome: I do.

Director: Peace as in something that soothes?

Handsome: Yes, exactly.

Director: Something like a lullaby?

Handsome: Well, I don't know if I'd go that far.

Director: Why not?

Handsome: You know why not. A lullaby is for children.

Director: It puts them to sleep?

Handsome: Yes.

Director: But don't you wish to sleep — in your lover's arms?

Handsome: Of course I do.

Director: What kind of music is good for that?

Handsome: Oh, it could be many kinds.

Director: Could it be rock music?

Handsome: I suppose some people can sleep to that.

Director: Because it rocks the cradle and lulls them to sleep?

Handsome: I'm glad you think you're very funny. But here's the thing. Typically rock music makes you want to move.

Director: Move together with your lover?

Handsome: Sure.

Director: How do lovers move when they're together?

Handsome: You know how they move.

Director: Would I know if I were amusical?

Handsome: You might, Director. So tell me how you move.

Director: Very carefully.

Handsome: Ha! I suppose you do. But really — isn't there a music that gets you moving?

83. MOVING

Director: What if I told you that there's no music that gets me moving — but that I watch my friends and lovers move to their own music and am inspired by them?

Handsome: Are you saying you don't feel their music?

Director: Right. I just watch and learn without even feeling the beat.

Handsome: And what do your friends think about this?

Director: Oh, they're always trying to get me to dance.

Handsome: Are you talking literally or metaphorically?

Director: Both.

Handsome: Well, literally — who cares? So you're not a good dancer. But metaphorically I have some concerns.

Director: What concerns?

Handsome: Name a dance they ask you to dance.

Director: Getting excited about things they're excited about.

Handsome: But you're not always excited.

Director: Correct.

Handsome: So do you pretend to be excited? Is that how you dance with them?

Director: Why, no. I gently, playfully tease them about their excitement.

Handsome: And that's your dance?

Director: That's my dance.

Handsome: And if you had to describe this dance in physical terms, how would you?

Director: I think this is a very old ethnic sort of dance. But here's how it goes. Everyone dances in a line. One of the line breaks off just as things are getting started and moves to a point on the floor where he can address the whole line. He teases the dancers in good fun. The line then bends around and encircles him, dancing around him again and again, shouting back playful yet mocking taunts. That's how I think it goes.

Handsome: You know, I can see that as your dance, see you in the middle.

Director: Does that answer your concerns?

Handsome: Yes, I suppose it does.

Director: But what about you?

Handsome: Me? I love to move to the music.

Director: Well, literally, I've got little concern about that. But metaphorically? Do you move to metaphorical music?

Handsome: You mean do I pretend to get excited about things I'm not excited about? I suppose I'm guilty of that from time to time. It's just being polite. But I think your way is better.

Director: Then why don't you playfully tease from time to time? Learn some different moves?

Handsome: Maybe I will.

84. THOSE SHOES

Director: I think you'd better have your moves ready for when you meet your love.

Handsome: Oh? And why is that?

Director: Because you're not always going to be excited about what she's excited about. Or do you think you will?

Handsome: Of course not.

Director: And what if she's excitable?

Handsome: Lively, you mean?

Director: Sure, lively. What then if you have no moves of your own? Will you just go along and fake excitement?

Handsome: No. Then the relationship starts to be a lie.

Director: What do you do?

Handsome: I sing a tune that harmonizes with her excitement.

Director: How will you do that? She's excited, and you're not. Where's the harmony?

Handsome: Let's say she's excited because she just bought some shoes. I could tease, saying: That's a beautiful pair of shoes; I wish I could fit into those shoes. She'll know I was teasing but will appreciate the compliment.

Director: So you'd say something that wasn't true. You'd lie.

Handsome: What do you mean?

Director: Do you really wish you could fit into those shoes?

Handsome: Why, no.

Director: So you lied.

Handsome: Okay, but that's the whitest of lies.

Director: I have one that's whiter, I think.

Handsome: Let's hear it.

Director: That's a beautiful pair of shoes; but they'll never fit me. See? Nothing untrue.

Handsome: Ah, but the 'but' is untrue. It suggests you want them to fit you.

Director: So tell me something better.

Handsome: That's a beautiful pair of shoes; and they'll never fit me.

Director: Yes, I suppose that is a bit better. I think you're learning your tune.

85. Excited By Excitement

Handsome: But something occurs to me.

Director: Oh? What?

Handsome: If my love is truly excited about her shoes, won't her excitement, the excitement itself — excite me?

Director: Well, it seems you have a point.

Handsome: Do you see anything wrong at my being excited about her excitement?

Director: Is she excited at your excitement?

Handsome: Yes, I think she is.

Director: And you'll be excited at her excitement for your excitement?

Handsome: Yes.

Director: And so on, and so on? Where does it end?

Handsome: Where do you think it will end?

Director: Exhaustion.

Handsome: But wouldn't it be a good sort of exhaustion?

Director: I can think of worse.

Handsome: Yes. But then something occurs to me. This is all fine — as long as what she's excited about doesn't bother me.

Director: Yes, shoes are easy.

Handsome: What if she's excited about something I oppose?

Director: What could you oppose?

Handsome: Let's say it's some sort of political opinion.

Director: Ah, then there might be trouble.

Handsome: Do you think it's better to keep politics out of the relationship?

Director: I don't see how you can.

Handsome: I could refuse to talk about politics when I'm around my love.

Director: And would you forbid her from doing the same?

Handsome: That seems a little harsh. Maybe I have to find a love that doesn't want to talk about politics, that doesn't care about politics.

Director: And you think that will make all your troubles go away? Tell me, Handsome. What kind of people aren't interested in politics?

Handsome: The smart kind?

Director: Are the smart kind those who let others manage their affairs?

Handsome: Of course not. The smart kind manage their own affairs.

Director: And yet politics is about, at some level, managing people's affairs. Are you and your love somehow exceptions?

Handsome: No, politics affects us.

Director: But you just won't talk about how it affects you. Is that it?

Handsome: No, I suppose we have to talk about it.

Director: How do you think politics affects you most?

Handsome: Let's say for the sake of argument that it's through taxes.

Director: Then tell me. Is this how you think of it? Money is the fuel of private life and the government seeks to siphon it off.

Handsome: That's exactly how I think of it.

Director: What's the most important part of your private life?

Handsome: My love.

Director: So if the government siphons off your money, it interferes with your love?

Handsome: Well, I don't like to say that.

Director: Why not?

Handsome: Because then we seem to suggest that love is based on money. And that's far from an exciting thought.

86. MONEY CAN'T

Director: Money can't buy love?

Handsome: No, it can't.

Director: But money can affect love?

Handsome: Money can put pressure on love.

Director: You mean the absence of money can put pressure on love.

Handsome: Yes.

Director: Are you sure?

Handsome: Very sure.

Director: But how can it do this? Does it take away the things you get excited about?

Handsome: No one is buying shoes when the money is gone.

Director: Then doesn't it seem you have to find other things to get excited about?

Handsome: Like what?

Director: Oh, I don't know. Couldn't you go to the library and find something there?

Handsome: At the library? Really?

Director: Haven't you ever read a good book, a book that excites you?

Handsome: I have.

Director: How many times did you read it?

Handsome: What do you mean?

Director: I mean, how many times did you read it?

Handsome: Once.

Director: Once? Only once? Why?

Handsome: What do you mean? I read the book and then I was done with it. But what about you?

Director: Oh, I read good books at least once every year.

Handsome: You find a new book every year?

Director: No, I mean I re-read each good book at least once each year.

Handsome: But why?

Director: Because they inspire me.

Handsome: But don't you ever get sick of your books?

Director: Sick of inspiration? Never.

Handsome: So that's the moral of the story.

Director: Tell me.

Handsome: My love and I should find things that inspire us, things that we can turn to again and again without tiring of them — and these things should be free.

Director: Yes. And if you can do that, if you can find inspiration in the free, then haven't you gone a long way toward making yourselves... free?

87. FREE

Handsome: But no one is ever truly free.

Director: Not even in the sense of free love?

Handsome: Ha! That's not love. That's just about the body.

Director: I thought it was about more than that. But what you care about is freedom of the spirit?

Handsome: Yes, of course.

Director: But you don't believe the spirit can truly be free?

Handsome: When I said 'no one is ever truly free' I meant always free.

Director: So our spirits are sometimes free and sometimes not.

Handsome: Yes.

Director: Why do you think that is?

Handsome: Because we all have our good days and our bad days.

Director: What if your love had more good days than bad days?

Handsome: Then I'd be happy.

Director: And if your love had more bad days than good?

Handsome: I'd try to do something about it.

Director: What would you do?

Handsome: I'd try to help lift her spirit and make it free once again.

Director: But what if it's just too heavy for you alone?

Handsome: Then I'd have to get help.

Director: What sorts of people would you enlist?

Handsome: Friends, family.

Director: And if it's too heavy for them? What about professional lifters?

Handsome: You mean psychologists and the like?

Director: Yes. Are you willing to employ them?

Handsome: If friends and family can't do the job? I think I have to be.

Director: And if your love doesn't want their help?

Handsome: Then I'd have to persuade her that it's best.

88. A New Dance?

Director: Suppose you do. Does it bother you if the professionals talk about your relationship with your love?

Handsome: No, I expect they would.

Director: And what if they conclude she needs to learn a new dance and they teach her how it goes?

Handsome: It's a dance to dance with me? Do I like this dance?

Director: No, not at all.

Handsome: Well, maybe I could learn to like it — for her sake.

Director: What if I told you that she doesn't like it, either?

Handsome: Maybe she has to learn to like it, too?

Director: Do you say that because you believe a new dance is in order?

Handsome: Something has to give her a lift.

Director: But what if it becomes clear that the dance the professionals suggest won't do the trick?

Handsome: I guess we have to get a second opinion.

Director: And if the new professionals recommend another dance that doesn't work?

Handsome: We try again with other professionals.

Director: And if again it doesn't work?

Handsome: I'm not the sort to give up, if that's what you're wondering.

Director: I know you're not. But maybe there's something you can do.

89. Touch

Handsome: What do you think I can do? I already tried to help lift her spirit and failed.

Director: Yes, but what if the professionals, though they didn't find the cure, gave you a pretty good idea of what the problem is?

Handsome: But even if I have that pretty good idea, I'm still not sure what I can do.

Director: You can use your touch.

Handsome: My touch? What are you talking about?

Director: When your love's spirit is free, how do you interact with her, essentially?

Handsome: I don't understand.

Director: Don't you touch her in her heart, touch her in her soul?

Handsome: Yes, of course.

Director: And does she respond to your touch? Does her spirit dance?

Handsome: Yes. But when her spirit isn't free, she doesn't respond or dance. That's the whole point, isn't it?

Director: Yes, but maybe you need to learn how to adjust your touch for when her spirit isn't free.

Handsome: And the professionals can give me an idea of how to do this?

Director: They can give you an idea of how to start.

Handsome: But once I start, what do I do then?

Director: You listen.

Handsome: But, Director, you know I would already be listening to her.

Director: Yes, but once you listen you have to speak, speak truth in response to what you hear.

Handsome: Again, that's something I would already do. But what do you think I'll hear?

Director: I don't know. You have to be ready for anything.

Handsome: And if she says nothing?

Director: Then you must speak truth and keep on speaking it until you get a response.

Handsome: Truth about what?

Director: The things that will help her spirit brighten and toughen.

Handsome: And what things are they? What truths?

Director: The truth about self. The truth about others. And the truth about life.

Handsome: Oh, is that all?

Director: Well, if it's too much for you....

Handsome: No, no. I'm not saying that. So where do we go from there, once we've talked all this through?

Director: You'll have to keep talking it through, over and over again.

Handsome: But if it's just talk and talk — what's the point?

Director: If you keep on speaking truth, and you listen closely when she responds to what you say — won't you start to have more than a pretty good idea of what it is that's getting her down?

Handsome: I suppose I will. I'll actually know what's getting her down.

Director: And once you know, you can try to help her take whatever it is away.

Handsome: Using my touch, the touch the professionals lacked.

Director: Yes.

Handsome: And if we succeed in taking it away, her sprit will rise and dance?

Director: If the two of you have truly worked the cure? Yes. But there's something I should mention.

Handsome: What, Director?

Director: You're trying to bring your mate the healing touch?

Handsome: Of course.

Director: Can you imagine a situation in which the literal touch, the physical touch, would interfere with the healing touch?

Handsome: Well, sometimes the literal touch is the healing touch. But, yes, I know what you mean. So you're saying no literal touch until things get better?

Director: You have to use your judgment. But remember this. Even when someone's spirits begin to lift, you have to be careful. A person in recovery is vulnerable. So even though she feels better, it still might not be time.

Handsome: So when would you say it's safe?

Director: When else, but when you're sure your love's spirit is both tough and bright?

90. WHAT IF

Handsome: But what if we're physical before then?

Director: And it interferes with the healing?

Handsome: Yes, let's say it does.

Director: Then you're not the man I thought you were.

Handsome: Oh, come on! I'm only asking hypothetically.

Director: Hypothetically? I think she might be better served by someone else.

Handsome: But isn't there a way for me to make up for my lapse?

Director: It's hard to say.

Handsome: Okay. But now let's flip things around. What if I told you I'm the one who needs to toughen and brighten?

Director: I'd tell you to find a lover who's like the lover you yourself would be.

Handsome: But if I'm not tough and bright, what sort of a lover would I be?

Director: I'm talking about what you would be at your best — not as you are at your worst.

Handsome: But how would I know what I'd be at my best?

Director: Don't you think everyone has an idea of how they'd be at their best?

Handsome: I don't know, Director. I think some people have no idea.

Director: Well, if you have no idea, my advice to you is to hold off on any relationships.

Handsome: What if I have an idea and it's a bad idea?

Director: Get rid of it.

Handsome: Sure, but how would I know it's bad except by trying it out in a relationship?

Director: Yes, but the problem with that is that you might get into a relationship with someone who knows how to take advantage of your bad idea.

Handsome: That's a good point. I'm not sure what happens then.

Director: I'll tell you what happens then. You're in a bad way.

Handsome: So what's to be done?

Director: No relationships until you can tell when you're being taken advantage of.

Handsome: But that's something some people never can tell.

Director: Then they'd better hope for some luck when it comes to a mate.

91. LUCK

Handsome: That's it? Hope for some luck?

Director: Isn't that how most people get through life?

Handsome: Yes, but I expect more from you.

Director: You expect I can teach potential lovers how not to be taken advantage of?

Handsome: Yes.

Director: Well, how do you think I'd start?

Handsome: By teaching self-confidence.

Director: And then?

Handsome: By making sure they have an idea of how they'd be at their best.

Director: And then?

Handsome: You could interview potential lovers, screen out those who want to take advantage.

Director: Why not just go on then and make the match myself?

Handsome: Why not? That would be better than relying on luck.

Director: Why's that?

Handsome: Because you know people better than most people do.

Director: And knowledge is better than luck?

Handsome: Of course it is.

Director: But what if you need both? In fact, don't you need both?

Handsome: Why do you need luck if you know what to find?

Director: I can tell just by listening to you that you're a handsome man with many choices when it comes to potential lovers.

Handsome: You're saying people need luck to find what they know they need — even when they have help from someone like you?

Director: Of course. And you need luck, too.

Handsome: I believe you. But tell me why.

Director: Because you don't know what you need.

Handsome: Really? What do I need?

Director: You'll think I'm evading the question when I say that I'll know when I see it.

Handsome: But if you'll know it, why won't I?

Director: You're too busy fending off all of those who are interested in you.

Handsome: So what are you suggesting? You'll just follow along at my side, ever on the lookout for my one true mate?

Director: In so many words? Yes. Between you, me, and our combined luck — things just might work out fine.

Handsome: I didn't know you can combine luck.

Director: There are a lot of things you don't know.

92. Ears, Eyes

Handsome: What else don't I know?

Director: About love? Well, since you don't know the most important thing — how to recognize your love — I'm not sure what point there is dwelling on the details.

Handsome: Maybe if I learn the details I'll learn the main thing?

Director: Maybe. So let's start with this. What's more important — the eyes or the ears?

Handsome: You mean on my potential mate?

Director: On both you and your potential mate.

Handsome: You want me to say the ears, because what we say is more important than how we look.

Director: I admit, I was inclined to say that. But now I'm not so sure.

Handsome: Why not?

Director: Do you want a mate you're not attracted to by the eyes?

Handsome: Honestly? No.

Director: No matter how many wonderful things the person in question says?

Handsome: I'm embarrassed to say it.

Director: Say it.

Handsome: No matter how many wonderful things the person says, if she doesn't please my eye I don't want her as my mate.

Director: And now the other way. No matter how pleasing she is to your eye, do you want her if she has nothing good to say?

Handsome: No.

Director: You want both eye and ear to be pleased.

Handsome: I do.

Director: Do you think there's anything wrong with that?

Handsome: No, I don't.

Director: Assuming you can't find someone perfectly pleasing in both respects, on which side do you err?

Handsome: Toward the ear.

Director: Are you just saying that because you think you'll please me?

Handsome: No. The ear is more easily offended than the eye. At least that's how it is with me. How is it with you?

Director: Me? I go by smell.

Handsome: Ha! But be serious.

Director: You think I'm kidding? If something smells funny, I don't want anything to do with it. Do you?

Handsome: Of course not.

Director: So the nose takes precedence over the eyes and the ears. Well, there — that's another thing you didn't know.

93. THE NOSE

Handsome: But you're speaking metaphorically.

Director: What if I am?

Handsome: Then you can tell me how you know something smells funny.

Director: The nose knows, my friend.

Handsome: But what's 'the nose'?

Director: Are you looking for a particular region of the brain that sniffs out trouble?

Handsome: Why are you reluctant to share what you know?

Director: I'm really not, Handsome. It's just that I don't know how I know. I just know.

Handsome: Does everyone just know?

Director: Some people do.

Handsome: And they're the ones most likely to find true love?

Director: Provided they're lucky.

Handsome: But haven't you heard that love makes you know?

Director: I have heard something like that. But what does it mean?

Handsome: When you find love, you just know.

Director: And you find love through luck, assuming you've got no nose to help you know?

Handsome: Well, yes.

Director: I'd rather just know through my nose and hope for a bit of luck than wait for a whole lot of luck to come along.

Handsome: But isn't luck luck?

Director: Of course it is. But we haven't talked about the odds. If you don't know what sorts of relationships smell funny, what do you think the odds are you'll find a good relationship? I mean, won't you waste time on bad relationships, time that could have been spent looking elsewhere?

Handsome: True.

Director: So what will you say are the odds?

Handsome: For finding true love without a good nose? Let's say they're one in a million.

Director: Okay. And now what do you think the odds are when you can tell right away what relationships are bad, so you don't waste any time on them?

Handsome: One in ten thousand?

Director: So luck isn't simply luck. Or rather, some things take more luck than others.

94. MEANT TO BE

Handsome: But regardless of the odds, a lot of people believe they will inevitably find their one true love, that it's simply meant to be.

Director: 'Meant to be.' What does that mean?

Handsome: It means regardless of what you do or don't do, it will happen.

Director: But haven't you heard people say: If it's meant to be, it's meant to be?

Handsome: Of course I have.

Director: What does that mean?

Handsome: It means it might not happen.

Director: So not everyone finds her or his one true love?

Handsome: Right. It might not be meant to be.

Director: But don't you believe we all have our one true love out there?

Handsome: I like to think that.

Director: Why?

Handsome: Why do I like to think that? Because it's nice to think that everyone can be happy.

Director: And finding your one true love always makes you happy?

Handsome: You don't think it does?

Director: I'm not sure. I mean, I see couples who look quite happy from time to time. But then I see people passionately in love who seem miserable more often than not.

Handsome: Well, maybe the passionate ones aren't each other's one true love.

Director: Not even if they're so passionate there's no way they could ever be more passionate?

Handsome: Director, there's a difference between being in love and being mad.

Director: What's the difference?

Handsome: Keeping things at a simmer rather than at a boil.

95. Simmers and Boils

Director: So if you meet someone and you start to boil inside, you know to stay away? And similarly, if you meet someone and she's boiling inside — stay away?

Handsome: Well, look. Here's the thing. Sometimes at first there's a great boil that later settles into a simmer.

Director: Is there any way of telling in advance that a certain boil might settle?

Handsome: Not that I'm aware of.

Director: Then why not take no chances and always go with a simmer when you can find one?

Handsome: Because simmers aren't as easy to see as boils.

Director: What? You mean if you meet a woman who's simmering away for you, you might not notice?

Handsome: Right. I might not.

Director: I find that very hard to believe for someone as sensitive as you, Handsome. But what about the other way? What if you're simmering for someone? Do you just ignore how you feel?

Handsome: But, Director, I always seem to be simmering for someone.

Director: Well, at least that's better than being up in a boil all the time.

Handsome: What do you think I can do?

Director: What's to be done? Is it bad to simmer?

Handsome: Simmering in itself isn't bad. But simmering all the time for different people? It drives me crazy! Besides, what am I going to do if I find my one true love — and I'm still simmering like this for others?

Director: One thing at a time. First, we have to deal with the fact that all your simmering drives you crazy. Second, we have to consider what all your simmering means for your one true love. And now that I think about it, I think I have an answer for both, an answer you'll like.

Handsome: What answer?

Director: That one of the ways you'll know you've found your one true love is that you stop simmering for everyone but her. And if you're crazy, at least you're only crazy for her.

Handsome: You mean that, in a sense, that's the definition of true love — you only simmer for that person? It's something that just happens, that can't be helped?

Director: That's the idea. What do you think?

Handsome: I truly hope that's how it works!

Director: Have you ever seen evidence to the contrary?

Handsome: Well, I have noticed that those who simmer together stay together. And can you stay together if you're simmering all over the place?

Director: No, that seems unlikely.

Handsome: So maybe it's true.

Director: Yes. Now what about the other way?

Handsome: What other way?

Director: The boil. Can you boil for anyone else if you've found your one true love?

Handsome: I'm afraid that's possible.

Director: What evidence do you see?

Handsome: Sometimes simmering couples break up over a great big boil.

Director: And what comes of the boil?

Handsome: Usually? Nothing. Unless....

Director: Unless?

Handsome: Unless the boil settles in to an exclusive simmer.

96. ONE AND ONLY ONE

Director: Now what are we saying? That someone moves from one true love to another?

Handsome: No, it doesn't work like that.

Director: So either the simmer you leave or the simmer you end up with isn't your one true love?

Handsome: Yes.

Director: Hmm. Then what would that mean about simmering?

Handsome: We said you wouldn't simmer for others if your love is true — you'd only simmer for The One.

Director: Yes, but now we're saying you thought you were in true love, simmering only for The One — and then along comes a boil that reduces to a simmer, and that this might be The One. And isn't it The One if you never simmer for anyone else, anyone at all?

Handsome: Well, it might be — as long as you don't succumb to another boil.

Director: Boils, yes. Then is it as simple as changing our definition?

Handsome: Tell me.

Director: True love is only true when neither simmer nor boil tempts you from your love.

Handsome: And the feeling is mutual.

Director: And the feeling is mutual. What do you think?

Handsome: I think it's true.

Director: But you've never felt true love.

Handsome: No, I'm always tempted by others.

Director: But you believe there's a one and only love out there for you?

Handsome: Yes, Director — I do.

97. Release

Director: You believe you want to simmer or boil for only one person for the rest of your life.

Handsome: Yes.

Director: Why?

Handsome: What do you mean?

Director: Why do you want that?

Handsome: Because I want to feel true love!

Director: I don't believe it.

Handsome: What? What are you talking about?

Director: I think you want to feel release.

Handsome: Well, isn't that part of true love? Release?

Director: Tell me what you want to be released from.

Handsome: The madness of love.

Director: Of simmers and boils?

Handsome: Yes.

Director: But won't you simmer and sometimes boil with your One?

Handsome: True.

Director: And will these simmers and boils that you'll feel with your One somehow differ from what you want to be released from?

Handsome: Of course they will.

Director: How? Will they be less intense?

Handsome: No.

Director: Will they occur less frequently?

Handsome: No. In fact, the simmers will be all but constant.

Director: Then where do we find this release you're talking about?

Handsome: The release comes when you stop trying to determine if your love is reciprocated. And not just partially reciprocated. But fully reciprocated.

Director: You want her temperature to be the same as yours.

Handsome: Yes.

Director: And madness ensues when it's not?

Handsome: That's right.

Director: Then is that the great release? Finding perfect reciprocation?

Handsome: That's the greatest of releases.

Director: But it's a strange sort of release.

Handsome: How do you figure?

Director: What, exactly, are you being released from?

Handsome: Worry. Anxiety.

Director: Couldn't you be freed of worry and anxiety another way?

Handsome: What other way?

Director: A way that may sound terrible.

Handsome: Well?

Director: Walk away from the love.

Handsome: No, that's not possible.

Director: Why not? If you're simmering or even boiling for someone, and you walk away, won't your temperature drop and your water grow calm?

Handsome: Yes, yes — of course. But why would you want to do that?

Director: Didn't we just say we wanted release from worry and anxiety? Will you be worried and anxious when your water is once again at room temperature?

Handsome: But you're asking the impossible!

Director: It's impossible to stop the madness?

Handsome: No, I don't mean that. I mean....

98. NO MADNESS HERE

Director: You mean you can't walk away from love.

Handsome: Yes.

Director: Why?

Handsome: Because what if it really is my one true love?

Director: I see. Well, why don't you try this?

Handsome: What?

Director: Walk away from this feeling of love. Walk far enough away that your water is calm. Then, slowly, walk back.

Handsome: Walk back?

Director: Yes. Walk back until you're just about at a simmer — and then walk away again.

Handsome: And let me guess. You want me to keep on doing this until I get some idea if there is any simmering on her part.

Director: Yes. Test it. Prove this love. And after many tries, if you feel an exclusive simmer for her, and you start to get the sense that she feels an exclusive simmer for you, a simmer that matches yours — approach her fully. Don't you think that's only smart?

Handsome: I do think that's only smart.

Director: No madness involved here?

Handsome: No, no madness involved here. But what if I boil for her?

Director: Isn't it the same process?

Handsome: I'm not sure.

Director: Why?

Handsome: Because if I get close enough to boil I might just rush right in.

Director: You have to steel yourself, my friend. Get far enough away that there's no boil. Then come close enough in for a simmer. And see how she reacts.

Handsome: Sure, Director. But all of this depends on a metaphor.

Director: What do you mean?

Handsome: The water heating when I draw near and cooling when I pull away. I mean, what if I long for her no matter how far away I am? That's what really makes for madness. I could go to the ends of the earth and still feel my longing. Do I just stay away?

Director: What's the alternative? To rush right in?

Handsome: They say fools rush in.

Director: Well, are they right?

Handsome: They might be. And I might be a fool. So maybe I should rush right in.

99. FOOLS

Director: But I don't believe you're a fool.

Handsome: What am I, then?

Director: You're a man inclined toward love.

Handsome: And what does that mean?

Director: It means you need to take care.

Handsome: Take care that I don't fall into bad relationships?

Director: Yes, but also care that you find good relationships.

Handsome: But why not just one good relationship?

Director: How likely are you to find the one perfectly good relationship if you haven't had the less than perfectly good? Tell me, Handsome. What do you think of the perfectly good?

Handsome: I think of it as an ideal.

Director: And when you have far less than the perfectly good, what happens to your ideal?

Handsome: It should shine all the more brightly as a beacon of hope — as long as I don't give up on it.

Director: And your ideal is perfect reciprocation?

Handsome: Yes.

Director: Do you think it's possible to believe there's perfect reciprocation in a relationship when in fact there isn't?

Handsome: Yes, you can be fooled for a while.

Director: What would prevent your being fooled?

Handsome: Having eyes to see.

Director: How do you train your eyes to see?

Handsome: Through experience.

Director: What's the best kind of experience?

Handsome: Mistakes?

Director: I was thinking it might be something else.

Handsome: What?

Director: Backing off from your love until your water is calm, then approaching once more, then backing off and approaching, and so on. I know you have concerns that this won't always work. But when it does, it's the kind of experience I think is best for training the eye. You learn to focus from different distances — and you see different things.

Handsome: And when my eyes are focusing properly and I see different things?

Director: You'll know what you're getting yourself into.

100. At First Sight, 2

Handsome: Do you think it's possible that if my eyes aren't trained I might actually find the perfect relationship but just not see it?

Director: Of course I think it's possible. You might not see the person for what she truly is.

Handsome: I might not appreciate her.

Director: Yes.

Handsome: So love isn't all about feeling.

Director: Can you say more?

Handsome: It's about seeing — knowing. You need to know the person for what she is.

Director: I agree.

Handsome: And the approaching and backing away helps you know.

Director: It no doubt can.

Handsome: But isn't there a risk you'll alienate her with all the approaching and backing away?

Director: I don't think it's much of a risk. If she's the kind of person you want, won't she be doing the same thing, trying to get to know you?

Handsome: I suppose that's true. But you know that phrase love at first sight? What if what it really means is knowledge at first sight — recognition? Do you think that's possible?

Director: Is it possible for both lovers to know the other at once, immediately? I think it happens. But it means they're prepared for the encounter well in advance.

Handsome: How are they prepared? Their eyes work well?

Director: Yes, their eyes work well — both internally and externally.

Handsome: What do you mean?

Director: They know how to look at others, and they know how to look at themselves.

Handsome: They know themselves.

Director: Put simply? Yes.

Handsome: So if you don't know yourself, at least the part of you that's not yet whole, you won't find love?

Director: True love? Probably not.

Handsome: Why?

Director: Because if you don't know yourself, you don't know what you need in a mate. If you don't know what you need in a mate, you're just stumbling around blindly trying to find it.

Handsome: That makes sense. But it's hard to concentrate on knowing yourself when you're pining away for love.

101. The Wrong Kind Of Love

Director: Instead of pining, or languishing, and so on — don't you think it would be better to long for love?

Handsome: What difference does it make?

Director: All the difference in the world.

Handsome: Tell me how.

Director: Pining and languishing imply weakness. Longing implies strength. Don't you agree?

Handsome: Strength because the desire is strong and you're strong enough to live up to your desire? I agree.

Director: Good. So you know never to allow yourself to waste away for love. If you must have love, then desire it with all your might.

Handsome: That sounds fine — until you start thirsting for love and there isn't a drop to be found.

Director: Yes, I take your point. Maybe this is where the other sort of love comes in.

Handsome: Love of family and friends? I'm sorry, Director, but if I'm longing for romantic love it might be nice, very nice indeed, to have the love of family and friends — but it's not enough.

Director: It's the wrong kind of love?

Handsome: Yes, it is.

Director: But it's love nonetheless?

Handsome: Of course it is.

Director: And that's something?

Handsome: Sure it is.

Director: Tell me. Would you agree that family and friends can help you know?

Handsome: Know? Know what?

Director: Yourself.

Handsome: Yes.

Director: And this knowledge can help you find love, romantic love, as we were just saying?

Handsome: True.

Director: And can't non-romantic love help you in another way?

Handsome: What way?

Director: The two types of love, romantic and non-romantic — are they entirely separate, or are there elements of the non-romantic in the romantic?

Handsome: As we said — there's overlap. Your true love is both family and friend to you, after all.

Director: So the more you know about the love of family and friends, the more you'll know about an important part of your romantic love?

Handsome: I suppose that's so.

Director: Then is it right to say that non-romantic love is simply the wrong kind of love for someone longing for romantic love?

Handsome: No, it's not.

102. THE LEAP

Director: So here we are with this strong desire for romantic love. And we want to be prepared for it when we find it. So we turn to our family and friends and try to learn as much as possible about non-romantic love as we can.

Handsome: This provides a sort of base, right?

Director: Right.

Handsome: But if we only know about non-romantic love, what do we do when we find romantic love?

Director: We make a leap.

Handsome: But you said we need to approach and retreat, approach and retreat.

Director: We do. But when we've done that enough, when our eyes are focusing correctly, when we know all we can know — we have to take a chance.

Handsome: You mean we have to decide whether to say, I love you?

Director: In essence? Yes. But what does it mean to say that?

Handsome: It means you share how you really feel.

Director: And once you start sharing how you really feel, what happens if you stop?

Handsome: The relationship withers.

Director: Now, let's suppose you take the leap — and your lover doesn't.

Handsome: That's not good.

Director: Is it good if she takes the leap and you don't?

Handsome: Of course not.

Director: Is what we're talking about related to the concept of reciprocated love?

Handsome: Certainly. Both lovers must leap, reciprocally.

Director: What if one lover is more comfortable leaping than the other?

Handsome: Then that lover must have patience.

Director: Suppose he or she has lots and lots of patience — but still no leap from the other.

Handsome: That could jeopardize the relationship.

Director: If everything else is right except for the leap, wouldn't it be a shame for the relationship to die?

Handsome: It would be a great shame.

Director: Tell me. Suppose the relationship eventually dies. Does that mean it wasn't true love? Do you know what I'm asking?

Handsome: I do. You're asking if true love can die, or whether, by definition, true love never dies.

Director: What do you think?

Handsome: I'm inclined to say that true love never dies; and that if the love died, that the other in this relationship wasn't The One.

Director: What if they meet again twenty years later and the one who wasn't ready to leap then is ready now?

Handsome: Well, it all depends on whether the other lover met The One in the meantime. If so, then the one who's ready now is out of luck.

Director: But if the other didn't meet The One?

Handsome: Then the one who's ready now should take the chance — and hope the other is still willing to leap.

103. THE ONES

Director: The notion of taking chances makes me wonder. We've spoken of The One several times. But what about the ones?

Handsome: What are you talking about?

Director: The ones along the way who lead you to The One. Shouldn't you be willing to take a chance on them?

Handsome: I suppose. Though I'd rather just meet my One right away.

Director: Who wouldn't? So what do you think we need to know about the ones?

Handsome: That each one gets better along the way.

Director: You mean, there's a sort of crescendo all the way up to The One?

Handsome: Yes.

Director: But does that always happen?

Handsome: No, I don't think it does.

Director: Why not?

Handsome: Because I think some people give up. And they settle for whatever they can get — even if they had better before.

Director: Do you think they admit to themselves the degree to which they're settling?

Handsome: I think some people do and some people don't.

Director: Which would be better?

Handsome: Which is better in a bad situation? I suppose it's best to be honest with yourself.

Director: That way if The One comes along you're ready?

Handsome: That sounds a little callous.

Director: Supporting true love is callous?

Handsome: It depends on how far you've settled, so to speak. If you're just dating someone, it's one thing. But if you're trying to build a life together? It's another.

Director: Suppose you're just dating. And then suppose along comes your One. And you're sure of it. You know it in your bones. What would you do?

Handsome: I would act in favor of true love.

Director: Whatever that would mean?

Handsome: Whatever that would mean.

Director: But it would be much easier if you had never settled, wouldn't it?

Handsome: Of course. But then maybe I wouldn't have found my One.

104. ENDING IT

Director: I wonder, Handsome. If you don't want to settle for less than your One, and you're in a casual relationship where it becomes clear you're not with your One — what would you do?

Handsome: End it.

Director: Right away?

Handsome: Right away.

Director: Even though it's only casual?

Handsome: Even so.

Director: But not everyone would do this, right?

Handsome: Of course. Some people always seem to need someone. And if they have someone, that's all they think they need.

Director: And that's a kind of settling, even though the relationship is casual?

Handsome: Yes.

Director: Do you think they're wasting their time?

Handsome: Without a doubt.

Director: Hmm. Have you ever told someone they should end a relationship?

Handsome: I have — and more than once.

Director: What did they say when confronted?

Handsome: Nothing good. They mumbled something about how it's fine for now.

Director: But what if it really is fine for now — for them?

Handsome: I can't see how it can be fine if it distracts them from looking for their One.

Director: That's because you have a strong desire for your One.

Handsome: And those who only care about 'fine for now' don't?

Director: Do you think they do?

Handsome: No. But that can't be all the difference between us and them.

Director: Why not?

Handsome: Because it's too simple.

Director: There are a lot of simple truths in this world.

Handsome: So what are you saying? The ones lacking strong desire shouldn't end their fine-for-now relationships?

Director: If they do, do you think they might find true love?

Handsome: They'll probably just end up in similar relationships once again. But I do think it's possible they can find true love — even though it's against long odds.

105. VIGOR

Director: Tell me, Handsome. Do you believe strong desire improves the odds?

Handsome: I do.

Director: And do you believe that if you couple vigor in the hunt with strong desire, you further improve the odds?

Handsome: Yes. And even if that doesn't improve the odds, I think it would make you feel better.

Director: How so?

Handsome: You always feel better when you do things with vigor.

Director: Is this another simple truth?

Handsome: I think it is. But I think people will say we're crazy.

Director: Why?

Handsome: Because who thinks of vigor when it comes to love?

Director: We do. Don't we count?

Handsome: Two people who have yet to find true love.

Director: Well, look at it this way. Can't we know a great deal about baseball without ever having played in the World Series?

Handsome: We can. But I don't know if it's the same way with love.

Director: Why not? Look at it like this. Can't a doctor know a great deal about a disease without ever having the disease?

Handsome: Now love is a disease?

Director: Let's switch it around. Can't a doctor know a great deal about healthy bodies without having a healthy body himself?

Handsome: Yes, he can.

Director: Then why can't we know a great deal about love?

Handsome: Maybe we can.

Director: At least we know one thing — strong desire for love and vigor in the hunt are beneficial. Don't we?

Handsome: I think that's two things.

Director: Then we know two things! Isn't that promising?

Handsome: It is. But tell me what exactly it means to be vigorous in the hunt.

Director: Mostly, it means to be full of energy and to search untiringly. And it means to be alert and to have strong presence of mind at all times on the odd chance that The One might appear. And it means to gently and thoroughly probe any potential One to determine if you should invest more time and energy in the person. Things along these lines.

Handsome: And you call that vigor?

Director: I call that vigor in the hunt. Why, what would you call it?

Handsome: I'd call it common sense.

106. COMMON SENSE

Director: What's the ultimate in common sense when it comes to love?

Handsome: The ultimate? I'd have to say it's recognizing your true love.

Director: Do you think it's an easy matter to recognize your true love?

Handsome: Well, since you've pointed out to me that I don't know how to recognize mine — no, I don't think it's always an easy matter.

Director: It sometimes takes an effort?

Handsome: Yes, I'd say it does.

Director: But who would believe us that this ultimate in common sense takes an effort to achieve? I mean, it's just common sense. No?

Handsome: Some things are easy for some people but hard for others, Director.

Director: How many people do you think have to make an effort for this kind of common sense, the ultimate common sense of love?

Handsome: I don't know how many, but I'd say that a lot of people lack common sense when it comes to love. In fact, they're crazy when it comes to love.

Director: And there's no common sense in being crazy.

Handsome: Of course not.

Director: What makes them crazy?

Handsome: When they feel love, romantic love, they lose their heads.

Director: They act like fools?

Handsome: Absolutely.

Director: What sorts of things do they do?

Handsome: They never stop talking about their love.

Director: What else?

Handsome: They stay up all night, tossing and turning, unable to sleep.

Director: Anything else?

Handsome: Oh, there are a million things. But here's the one that bothers me most. They allow themselves to be hurt.

Director: And it's just common sense not to allow yourself to be hurt.

Handsome: Right.

Director: How do they get hurt?

Handsome: They have feelings for those who don't share their feelings.

Director: Can they control their feelings?

Handsome: Who can do that?

Director: So they're simmering and maybe even boiling?

Handsome: They are.

Director: Then why don't they just walk away?

Handsome: That's the thing that gets me. They should — but they don't. They do the opposite.

Director: Even though everything says the other doesn't share their feelings?

Handsome: Exactly.

Director: Well, that's crazy. What do you think prevents them from walking away?

Handsome: I don't know. Maybe they had no practice doing it? And then love came up and attacked?

Director: Maybe. But how much practice do you need to turn around and walk away?

Handsome: Yes, I know what you mean.

Director: You've never done it? Stayed longer than you should when your water was hot?

Handsome: No, I have.

Director: Then what were you thinking?

Handsome: I wasn't. That's the point.

Director: I think you lacked knowledge.

Handsome: What kind of knowledge?

Director: Knowledge about yourself and what sort of match is right for you.

Handsome: Yes, I think that's true.

Director: So you know what we can say about these crazy people who keep their water hot for those who are cool to them, don't you?

Handsome: No, what?

Director: They're really not crazy — they just don't know what they need to know.

107. IGNORANT

Handsome: Yes, they're ignorant.

Director: Can we teach the ignorant about themselves and what sort of match is right for them?

Handsome: I don't know, Director. Isn't that knowledge you have to come to on your own?

Director: But if we see someone acting like a crazy man, boiling away for someone who doesn't want anything to do with him — can't we say, Look, you're acting like a crazy man?

Handsome: We can say it, but I don't know how much good it will do.

Director: What might do some good?

Handsome: Showing him someone who's interested in him.

Director: You mean we find him a one, not to say The One, and then tell him to get to work?

Handsome: Yes.

Director: And even if it's only a one, still, he can learn from the experience, the relationship — can't he?

Handsome: He can. But will he?

Director: Why wouldn't he?

Handsome: He might never step back to get a better view.

Director: He'll rush right in?

Handsome: Yes. And he'll get all in a boil and not pay any attention to what he's doing.

Director: Maybe we have to pull him back and coach him a little?

Handsome: I'm not sure he'll listen.

Director: So what's the best thing that could happen in this situation?

Handsome: The best? I hate to say it. But I think it's best if the other breaks things off.

Director: And why is that best?

Handsome: Because the pain our ignorant friend will feel might force him to reflect. To learn. To know.

108. PAIN

Director: Is learning always painful?

Handsome: When it comes to love? Not necessarily.

Director: You can have a pleasant time with someone you eventually break up with and learn from the experience?

Handsome: I think that's true.

Director: What do you learn?

Handsome: You learn this person isn't The One. And you learn what traits they lack that might have made them The One. And you remember these traits as you're looking for your One.

Director: So you create a sort of checklist.

Handsome: Yes, a list of what you want.

Director: And you can list what you don't want, too, I suppose.

Handsome: Of course.

Director: If it's that simple, why doesn't everyone learn this way?

Handsome: Because they're blinded by a certain pleasure.

Director: Oh? What pleasure?

Handsome: You know. Sex.

Director: Does this mean they're prone to falling into the same old trap over and over again?

Handsome: Yes, they seem doomed to fail — unless they open their eyes.

Director: Well, what can we do to help them?

Handsome: I'm afraid not much.

Director: Why?

Handsome: Because they're enjoying themselves.

Director: Really? Tell me, Handsome. Is it possible that some of these people enjoy only one thing in their relationship, their physical intercourse?

Handsome: Yes, certainly.

Director: And if they enjoy only that one thing, and that thing is fleeting — what will they be left with the rest of the time?

Handsome: Not much.

Director: Do they enjoy the 'not much'?

Handsome: No.

Director: Might we even say the 'not much' brings pain?

Handsome: You mean like the pain of jealousy?

Director: Sure, or of boredom or of annoyance or of quarrels or of harsh words.

Handsome: It does bring such pains.

Director: And are these pains fleeting or of a more lasting nature?

Handsome: Lasting.

Director: So we're saying these people have fleeting pleasure and lasting pain. Is that enough to say 'they're enjoying themselves'?

Handsome: No, it's not.

Director: So how can we help them?

Handsome: I guess we tell them what we're saying here — that we know they're not really enjoying themselves.

Director: And that's because they don't have real love?

Handsome: Exactly.

Director: And no amount of pleasure from the physical can make up for this fact?

Handsome: There's not enough pleasure in the world.

109. BEAUTIFUL

Director: Now, for real love we need real beauty. Don't we?

Handsome: Of course.

Director: And real beauty should never, in and of itself, bring pain.

Handsome: I agree. But haven't you heard people talk about things that are painfully beautiful?

Director: I have. But I can only guess that the beauty of those things somehow stirs up painful emotions in certain types of souls.

Handsome: I'm not sure I follow. Can you give an example of what you mean?

Director: Suppose someone who settled for a one sees a beautiful movie about finding true love. Painfully beautiful? It might well be.

Handsome: So if beauty shouldn't be painful, are you saying that those who experience it as such have done something wrong, made a mistake?

Director: Let's take the beautiful movie again. But this time, suppose the person in the audience lost their love, true love, to an illness. In other words, the person didn't do anything wrong. Could the movie be painful?

Handsome: It doesn't have to be.

Director: Tell me how.

Handsome: The movie might bring some relief from the pain of loss through its wonderful portrayal of finding true love. It might bring back beautiful memories.

Director: And these memories would bring pleasure?

Handsome: Yes.

Director: Can we say that all beautiful things should bring pleasure?

Handsome: I think that's the only thing that makes sense.

Director: What if I see the movie and feel no pleasure? What does that mean?

Handsome: It means the movie isn't beautiful to you.

Director: To me? You mean, some things are beautiful to some people and other things are beautiful to others?

Handsome: Of course.

Director: Is it the same with the opposite of beauty? The ugly?

Handsome: I'm not sure.

Director: Well, if the beautiful brings pleasure, what does the ugly bring?

Handsome: Pain.

Director: Should it bring pain?

Handsome: I have to say yes.

Director: How does this apply to people?

Handsome: You mean should beautiful people bring us pleasure and ugly people bring us pain?

Director: That's what I mean. What do you think?

Handsome: But that's a terrible thing to say.

Director: Did you think I was just talking about the body?

Handsome: You're talking about the whole person?

Director: Yes.

Handsome: Then, yes, beautiful people do bring us pleasure while ugly people bring us pain.

Director: Now, for the sake of argument, let's go back to the body. Should beautiful bodies bring us pleasure and ugly bodies bring us pain?

Handsome: Of course not.

Director: But do they in fact?

Handsome: When I see someone who's physically ugly, I don't feel any pain.

Director: But when you see someone who's physically beautiful?

Handsome: Well....

Director: Well?

Handsome: Maybe a little pleasure.

Director: Tell me honestly now. Is it a pleasure connected in some way to sex, or is it something else?

Handsome: It's something else. But I think it would be hard to explain exactly what that something is.

110. Something Else

Director: I wonder if it's like this. When you go to a museum and see a beautiful statue of a beautiful woman, do you feel pleasure?

Handsome: I do.

Director: What kind of pleasure?

Handsome: The 'something else' kind of pleasure.

Director: What is it about the statue that makes you feel that kind of pleasure?

Handsome: It has beautiful proportions. It has symmetry. It has my ideal of what a beautiful woman should look like.

Director: So it's the presentation of this ideal that brings you pleasure.

Handsome: Yes.

Director: And when you see a beautiful living human figure, one with beautiful proportions, and symmetry, and whatever else goes into your ideal — does this bring you pleasure?

Handsome: It does.

Director: Is it the same kind of pleasure as with the statue?

Handsome: In essence? Yes.

Director: But is that the only kind of pleasure you feel?

Handsome: You're asking if I'm immune to the charms of sex?

Director: Are you?

Handsome: Of course not. But I focus on the ideal.

Director: Do you ever let the two blend?

Handsome: Well, that's where it gets complicated.

Director: How so?

Handsome: Ideally, the two only blend in my One. But sometimes I think a one is my One.

Director: Yes, I can see how that might cause trouble. So it's a good thing this is all just a matter of secondary importance.

Handsome: How do you mean?

Director: Handsome, don't you know? I know you know. You're just forgetting that the beauty of the body is always less beautiful — than the beauty of the soul.

111. SOUL

Handsome: Of course. But what about the Me?

Director: You can love the Me. But I'm afraid you need to see more than just the good in a person. You need to see it all.

Handsome: So when I see a beautiful woman walking down the street, I should be looking out for her soul, her all?

Director: Without a doubt.

Handsome: And how will I catch sight of that?

Director: Maybe she's walking with someone and talking. You can see some of her soul come through in that. In fact, if you practice, you can learn to see a lot of a person's soul in the briefest of encounters.

Handsome: If I practice? You want me to become a stalker?

Director: Of course not. But don't you think you should pay attention to those around you?

Handsome: But what if some of them aren't worth my attention?

Director: How will you know they're not unless you pay them some attention first?

Handsome: So everyone deserves my attention, however briefly?

Director: Just as you deserve theirs.

Handsome: What if I don't want their attention?

Director: It doesn't matter if you do or if you don't. You'll get it all the same.

Handsome: But not from everyone.

Director: No, not from everyone. Some people are too self-absorbed.

Handsome: What if I see a beautiful woman, body and soul, and she's self-absorbed?

Director: You could find a polite way to approach her.

Handsome: And what would I say?

Director: My, what a beautiful soul you seem to have. I'd like to get to know you in order to see if it's as good as it seems.

Handsome: No, I didn't ask what you would say. I asked what I would say!

Director: Hello, I think you might be a one with long odds at being The One.

Handsome: Can't you be serious?

Director: You're going to have to work this out on your own. But I can recommend one thing.

Handsome: What?

Director: Try to find out what makes her self-absorbed.

Handsome: And if it's that she has a crisis in her soul?

Director: Then your mission is to see if there's a way you can help put the crisis to an end.

Handsome: And if I can do that? If I can help?

Director: Then you just might be one step closer to The One.

Handsome: You mean she might be The One?

Director: Maybe. But even if not, she might be able to help.

112. Help

Handsome: Just because someone is pretty and formerly crisis-ridden doesn't mean she can help.

Director: Oh, she's just pretty now? I thought she was beautiful.

Handsome: She'd be beautiful if she actually brought me toward my One.

Director: Ah, you're saying something interesting. Can you mean what I think you mean?

Handsome: What do you think I mean?

Director: You mean that I'm beautiful.

Handsome: Stop it.

Director: But I'm trying to bring you toward your One! Aren't you suggesting that anyone who helps you with that is beautiful?

Handsome: Well, yes, I suppose. But there's more to it than that.

Director: What more?

Handsome: It's not enough just to be brought to your One. You have to learn along the way. So you're prepared when you meet.

Director: And you're not learning from me?

Handsome: Alright, Director. You're beautiful. You're the most beautiful man I've ever seen. Happy?

Director: I want you to mean it. But that's a start. So tell me. What do you think you might learn from the beautiful and formerly self-absorbed woman? How will she help you, assuming she's not The One?

Handsome: I don't know.

Director: Well, look at it this way. What did you suggest was the cause of her self-absorption?

Handsome: A crisis in her soul.

Director: And I suggested it might be possible to help. Do you think I was being overly optimistic?

Handsome: No, I think it's possible to help.

Director: When isn't it possible?

Handsome: When it's not a crisis. When the self-absorption is due to pure and simple narcissism.

Director: So if it seems possible to help, you can be pretty sure what you're dealing with?

Handsome: Right.

Director: Well, now we can say how she can help you. Aren't you curious?

Handsome: Of course I'm curious. Tell me.

Director: But I'm afraid you won't like what she has to offer.

Handsome: Why are you stalling? Tell me what it is.

Director: Knowledge of crisis. I mean, she lived through a crisis, didn't she?

Handsome: Yes. But how can that knowledge help me?

Director: Now I'm afraid you'll like things even less.

Handsome: Why?

Director: Because before you have your answer, she wants to ask you a few questions.

113. Clues

Handsome: You mean you want to ask me a few questions first.

Director: She wants to ask. I want to ask. Judge for yourself who wants what. So let's begin. How did you help end my crisis?

Handsome: Why would she ask me that? Doesn't she know?

Director: Of course she does. But she's not so sure that you do.

Handsome: Well, I don't know how I helped end the crisis.

Director: But how, she asks, could you not know?

Handsome: I just... don't know!

Director: Then why did you approach me?

Handsome: Why did I approach her, Director?

Director: Ah, you're ruining the dialogue. But I'll tell you. You approached her because of something you saw that she had inside. Say it.

Handsome: I approached you because of something I saw that you had inside.

Director: What was this something?

Handsome: I honestly don't know.

Director: Then why did you seem to want me to nurture it all the same?

Handsome: I knew it was good.

Director: Well, that knowledge was enough.

Handsome: That's really all it took to help?

Director: That's really it.

Handsome: But now I'm afraid I don't deserve much in return.

Director: No, you deserve a great deal.

Handsome: What will you give me?

Director: I'll offer you a clue by way of thanks.

Handsome: What sort of clue?

Director: A clue about your One.

Handsome: I couldn't ask for more. So what's the clue?

Director: A woman you help with her crisis can never be your One unless she helps resolve the crisis in you.

Handsome: That's good advice.

Director: Now I, Director, want to know if you'd be happy to go around collecting such clues from beautiful women.

Handsome: I would. But no matter how happy that makes me I want the thing that will make me happier still.

Director: You want your true love.

Handsome: Yes.

Director: Well, gather your clues, and see where they lead, and then....

Handsome: And then I'll make a leap into the arms of my One! And that, Director, will make all the effort it took to find the right clues — that will make it good.

114. MAKE GOOD

Director: Yes, I know what you mean. But you'll need more good than that.

Handsome: What good will I need?

Director: The kind of good that makes everything you touch good.

Handsome: What, like the ancient king who turns all he touches to gold?

Director: In a sense? Yes.

Handsome: Now you're sounding crazy. Why would I need to make everything I touch good?

Director: Don't you know? The world doesn't go away just because you find your One. You need to make your world, the small part of the world that touches on you and your love — you need to make it good.

Handsome: Of course I'd like to do that. But what if I can't? Do you think our little world will tear our love apart?

Director: Do you think it will?

Handsome: If our love is true? No, nothing can tear us apart.

Director: Spoken like one who's always been a darling of the world.

Handsome: Look, I know that times can get tough — very tough. But isn't love what sustains us through those times?

Director: You're talking once again about a mighty powerful love.

Handsome: I wouldn't settle for, and I don't deserve, anything less.

Director: Then we must find you the One you need.

115. WHERE AND HOW

Handsome: Where shall we start?

Director: We've already started.

Handsome: Then let me ask — where shall we go now?

Director: Where do you think we might find your love? Do you have a hunch?

Handsome: A museum?

Director: Hmm. Maybe. But is there a better place?

Handsome: A park on a beautiful day?

Director: Could be. Can you think of anything else?

Handsome: How about one of those dating services?

Director: That might work. You can be very creative in describing yourself and your interests. And if you come across someone equally creative, well, that just might work.

Handsome: How should I describe myself? I mean, I can say I like to hike, and I have two dogs, and so on, and so on. But how do I describe me, my essence?

Director: Your essence? That's a tall order for a dating service. But let's see. Maybe you say what your favorite book is?

Handsome: Okay.

Director: And maybe you say that you like to talk philosophy with me?

Handsome: Well, maybe.

Director: Ah, ashamed of Director, are you?

Handsome: It's just that it'll sound kind of weird.

Director: Weird that you like to have long, meaningful conversations with a friend?

Handsome: No, not so weird, I guess.

Director: Remember, Handsome — the beginning is half of the whole. If you're embarrassed at the start about things that are important to you, I think you're in for trouble.

Handsome: I agree. My favorite book, our dialogues. What else?

Director: I'd focus more on the dialogues.

Handsome: Of course you would. How will I do that?

Director: You could take down snippets of our conversations and include them in your description of yourself.

Handsome: I think a lot of women would feel threatened by you if I do that.

Director: Do you want a woman who's threatened by your friends?

Handsome: No, you have a point. Okay. So let's say I do it. Let's say I write down tonight a summary of what we talked about today.

Director: A summary?

Handsome: Yes, a summary. Or do you really think I can remember all of what we say verbatim?

Director: A summary it is, then. Well, I wonder what sort of woman you'll reel in with this sort of bait. Oh, but there's one thing.

Handsome: What?

Director: You have to refuse to put a picture of yourself in your profile.

Handsome: Why?

Director: You don't want any of the fishies biting just because you're cute.

116. Scaring Them Off

Handsome: So I'm basically relying on a book and my conversation with you.

Director: I think your prospects are excellent. But maybe I could see the summary you write before you submit it?

Handsome: Ha! You don't trust me to faithfully reproduce the gist of our conversation.

Director: I just don't want you waxing poetic about The One.

Handsome: And why not? Isn't that what I'm looking for?

Director: Yes, but you want your potential mate to see you have a clear head when it comes to these things.

Handsome: Fine. I'll show you what I write. Satisfied?

Director: Almost.

Handsome: What more do you want?

Director: I really think you should include a bit of dialogue, after the summary, to give some flavor for the thing — even if you can't remember it verbatim. A summary alone just isn't enough.

Handsome: You just want to scare off the faint hearted.

Director: Well, there's some truth in that.

Handsome: Alright. That's what I'll do. I'll add some flavor. It'll be interesting to see who turns up.

Director: Yes. But tell me in all truth, Handsome. If someone shows up with a wonderful soul, but her physical appearance is, well, not great — will you turn her away?

Handsome: I'll try to learn from her. But I'll be honest and won't mislead her in any way.

Director: So you're aiming for that lucky occurrence of a happily constituted body and a happily constituted soul?

Handsome: Yes. That's why I find it hard to think I can't include a photo.

Director: Yes, the handsome always find that hard.

Handsome: But I'm serious. It will, sort of, you know... warn certain women off.

Director: Ha! You're saying, Look, I'm a handsome guy. So unless you're a beautiful woman, on the outside, don't bother.

Handsome: You scare off some, and I'll scare off the rest.

Director: Well, maybe that's best.

Handsome: Yes. And this way I'll increase my chances of finding someone who's right, someone who's right for me.

117. Mistake, Next Step

Director: But now I think we might be making a great mistake.

Handsome: How so?

Director: What if your picture scares off the wrong person?

Handsome: What person?

Director: A woman who looks plain in a photo, at best. But a woman who when you interact with her in person is quite beautiful. Would you want to be with someone like that?

Handsome: If she's truly beautiful? Yes, of course.

Director: But what if she's self-conscious about her looks in general and her photo in particular? And when she looks at your photo she thinks, Oh, someone like that would never be interested in me. Might she not pass you by?

Handsome: She might.

Director: But if she just focuses on what you say about yourself?

Handsome: She might be intrigued.

Director: Then will you leave the picture out and not distract her from what's important?

Handsome: Fine. I'll leave it out.

Director: Good.

Handsome: But I wouldn't be surprised if no one responds to me.

Director: You don't think there are women with fine minds out there who will be interested in what you set down in your profile?

Handsome: Do women with fine minds use dating services?

Director: Oh, I think they do. You have a fine mind and you're about to use a dating service.

Handsome: Alright. Let's say I meet someone with potential. What do I do? What's the next step?

Director: Really, Handsome. You keep speaking as if you have no experience with women. But here's what I think you should do. Bring her to meet me.

Handsome: Of course that's what you think I should do.

Director: Why not? Isn't the opinion of your good friend important?

Handsome: Yes, it's important.

Director: Are you worried I'll be rude?

Handsome: Of course not.

Director: Are you worried I'll scare her off?

Handsome: No, somehow I think the written dialogue she'll have seen is scarier than you in person.

Director: Why do you think that is?

Handsome: Because you have a gentle way.

118. GENTLENESS

Director: Gentleness is very important in a relationship, don't you think?

Handsome: I certainly do.

Director: What's one of the benefits of gentleness?

Handsome: You're free to think and then to say what you think.

Director: Harshness discourages thought and the speaking of thoughts?

Handsome: Of course it does. When someone is harsh you don't trust that they'll listen and consider what you have to say. That fact makes it less likely that you'll actually think.

Director: Hmm. I'm not sure about that. If someone were harsh to me I'd do a great deal of thinking — about how to get away from that person. But then again, maybe it would be different.

Handsome: What do you mean?

Director: What if the person is harsh but always speaks the truth? Should we try to escape?

Handsome: Well, it depends. Does this harsh person actually stop being harsh long enough to listen to what we have to say?

Director: Yes, let's say she does. She listens. She thinks about what we've said, then, harshly, she tells us what she thinks about it.

Handsome: I think we'd be wrong to run away from someone like that, from the truth.

Director: Would you consider this person to be a potential mate?

Handsome: Well, not running away is one thing. Getting into a relationship with someone like that is another.

Director: Why?

Handsome: Who can take that harshness all the time?

Director: So maybe you need to amend your profile.

Handsome: What, to say I'm looking for someone gentle?

Director: Yes.

Handsome: Alright. That's what I'll do.

119. ANYTHING ELSE?

Director: And while you're at it, why not specify any other traits you're looking for?

Handsome: Well, let's see. There's a strong heart.

Director: And?

Handsome: Intelligence.

Director: What else?

Handsome: Beauty of mind.

Director: Anything else?

Handsome: I can't think of anything else.

Director: You really can't think of anything else?

Handsome: Well, of course, there are the standard virtues. Honesty. Integrity. Fairness. You know.

Director: So you're just going to say, I'm looking for a gentle soul with a strong heart, intelligence, and beauty of mind — and oh yes, she has to have the standard virtues, too!

Handsome: Tease all you want, Director. But, you know, now that we're talking about it — I don't see why we can't count strength of heart and beauty of mind among the standard virtues. What do you think?

Director: I suppose there's nothing to stop us from doing so. But what about intelligence?

Handsome: What about it?

Director: Do you think we can count it among the standard virtues?

Handsome: I don't know. That doesn't sound right.

Director: What if you train your intelligence a certain way, a virtuous way?

Handsome: Well, that's how you arrive at a beautiful mind.

Director: So even if intelligence isn't a virtue, its proper use leads to virtue?

Handsome: Yes.

Director: What leads us to use intelligence well?

Handsome: I'm not sure I understand what you mean.

Director: I'm just wondering what guides us.

Handsome: Oh. But I feel foolish.

Director: Why?

Handsome: Because the only thing I can think is that you train the intelligence the way that a parent trains a child.

Director: If that's how it is, who plays the role of parent?

Handsome: Who do you think?

Director: What if I told you the whole world plays that role?

Handsome: The whole world conspires to train the intelligence?

Director: I suppose that sounds a bit ridiculous.

Handsome: Yes, but maybe it's because you overstated the case.

Director: What do you mean?

Handsome: I mean, maybe it's a quarter of the world, or a tenth.

Director: The tenth that's virtuous? Maybe so. But what do they teach?

Handsome: That's a good question. What do you think?

Director: Two things come to mind. But I'm not sure how well they go together.

Handsome: What's the first?

Director: Self-control.

Handsome: No, I'm not sure that's it. I mean, yes, we want people to have self-control. But is self-control really associated with the exercise of the intelligence? We want to use our intelligence to the full, not rein it in. What's the second thing that came to mind?

Director: Critical thinking.

Handsome: Now that sounds like more the thing.

Director: Do you think critical thinking is good?

Handsome: Of course I do. Everyone does.

Director: Everyone? Hmm. Maybe everyone would agree it's good in theory, but how about in practice?

Handsome: You're wondering about people who stifle thought, who stifle free inquiry?

Director: Yes. You do agree there are such people, don't you?

Handsome: Of course I do.

Director: Do you think they think critically?

Handsome: Definitely not.

Director: And when they encounter people who do?

Handsome: It bothers them — it bothers them a great deal.

Director: Now, you don't want someone like this as a mate.

Handsome: Are you kidding? No, I want someone who thinks.

Director: But you know the problem, don't you?

Handsome: Sure. If I put down that I'm looking for someone who thinks, I'll get lots of people who think — but only within a narrow range.

Director: And you want someone who thinks more broadly than that.

Handsome: Yes, of course.

Director: Then what's one more trait you need to ask for?

Handsome: I'll have to say I'm looking for someone with an open mind.

120. NEED TO KNOW

Director: What do we mean by an 'open mind'?

Handsome: We just mean that you're willing to consider different things.

Director: Different things than what you're used to considering?

Handsome: Yes.

Director: And the point is to get familiar with them?

Handsome: Right. But familiarity isn't enough.

Director: What more do you need?

Handsome: You really have to know them. You have to see them for what they are.

Director: And then?

Handsome: Then you can judge whether they're good for you.

Director: I see. But let's back up a step. Are you saying you can be familiar with something without knowing it?

Handsome: Of course. Here's an example. Your computer. You might use it every day. Wouldn't you say you're familiar with it?

Director: Sure.

Handsome: But you might not know what makes it up — the hardware, the software. So you don't really know it for what it is.

Director: But of course you do. Suppose you write books with your computer. You know the computer is a book writing machine. And that might be all you need to know, that it's good for that.

Handsome: But what you 'need to know' and what something 'is' are two different things.

Director: Is that always so?

Handsome: Yes, of course.

Director: Even in the case of love?

Handsome: Well....

Director: Why do you seem like you don't agree?

Handsome: Because in the case of love what you need to know and who the person is are the same.

Director: And it's only when you know who the person is, in the sense of your example with the computer, that you can judge whether she's good for you or not?

Handsome: Well, not exactly.

Director: What do you mean?

Handsome: I can know someone isn't good for me without knowing her in depth.

Director: But if you don't know, how do you know?

Handsome: I just know.

Director: But does it work the other way? Can you 'just know' someone is good for you without knowing her in depth?

Handsome: No, I'd need to know her in depth.

Director: Interesting. But even if you know someone in depth, how do you know if she's good for you?

Handsome: Do you remember when you mentioned having a checklist? I think it helps to have one here.

Director: And that's how you'd decide?

Handsome: I know. It sounds too simple. But isn't the simplest sometimes best?

121. What's Good For Me

Director: Yes, that's true. And the simplest of questions is: What's good for me?

Handsome: I agree.

Director: But tell me, Handsome. What if you're distracted and forget about this simple question?

Handsome: And how do you think that might happen?

Director: Maybe you should tell me.

Handsome: Ha! I know why you want me to tell you — because it's the beauty of the body that has the power to make us forget.

Director: The beauty of the body including the face?

Handsome: Yes, including the face.

Director: But the face is somehow different than the rest of the body, isn't it?

Handsome: It's more expressive.

Director: Can we say the face mirrors the soul?

Handsome: Yes, we certainly can say that.

Director: And you don't want a good body with a bad soul.

Handsome: Of course I don't.

Director: So if we know what's good for us, what will we do?

Handsome: We'll pay great attention to the face.

Director: And if we want to catch more than a flash of a reflection of the soul in the face, what must we do?

Handsome: We must talk. And we must listen closely to what the other says.

Director: Listen. Yes. I wonder if you believe what I'm inclined to believe.

Handsome: What are you inclined to believe?

Director: That the soul, though mirrored in the face, actually lives in words. The words we believe. The words we think. The words we speak.

Handsome: You think the soul is words?

Director: I'm not sure I'd say it's words, as in made up of words. But I often think it lives in words. Do you see the difference?

Handsome: I'm not sure I do.

Director: Well, that's a conversation for another time. But we agree words are very important?

Handsome: Very.

Director: What would happen if you showed someone your checklist and asked her to comment on it, in her own words?

Handsome: Don't you think that might be a little rude?

Director: Rude? Why?

Handsome: Because then she might feel compelled to show she lives up to the list!

Director: Not if she doesn't like you.

Handsome: True.

Director: But what if she pulls out a list of her own and hands it to you?

Handsome: We both have lists?

Director: Yes. Maybe you could warn her. Tell her, I'm bringing a list of things that are important to me in another, things that I think are good for me — would you mind doing the same?

Handsome: Well, that wouldn't be rude, at least. And it could make for some interesting conversation.

Director: So would you be willing to do something like that?

Handsome: Sure. Why not?

122. WHY NOT

Director: Now tell me, Handsome. What happens if you both work your way through your checklists and find that you each satisfy all that's on the other's list?

Handsome: Everything?

Director: Everything. But for one thing.

Handsome: What?

Director: There's no spark.

Handsome: You mean there's no real attraction?

Director: Yes.

Handsome: Then that's the end of that. No spark, no relationship.

Director: What I want to know is how there can be everything else, everything that you think is good for you — but there isn't love?

Handsome: I'm afraid there's no accounting for love.

Director: Why? Are people that unknowable?

Handsome: You can know people but not know what makes them feel a spark.

Director: Then let me ask you this. If you go on a date, and each of you brings a checklist, and you find that almost nothing gets checked, but you find that there's a spark, a clear attraction — what do you do?

Handsome: I see if we can't kindle a steady burning flame.

Director: Steady burning, yes. That's really the trick, isn't it?

Handsome: Of course. I've had my share of arsonists of the heart. They light a blaze and then when everything is burned to the ground they walk away. Well, I don't want a blaze. I just want a steady flame. One that's always with me, whatever I'm doing, wherever I am.

123. SPARKS

Director: So what do you do, Handsome, just go around looking for that certain spark that will light the steady burning flame?

Handsome: In so many words? Yes.

Director: And there really is no accounting for this spark? You find it when you find it?

Handsome: I'm afraid so.

Director: So is it all just blind trial and error? Spark after spark, hoping for the one that lights the flame?

Handsome: No, the checklist can help — even though it isn't always right.

Director: Because the checklist is designed around the idea of your flame? Around the idea of kindling that steady burning flame?

Handsome: Right. Without a spark there's no flame. But just because there's a spark it doesn't mean there will be a flame, the flame I want.

Director: So you have to be willing to turn sparks away.

Handsome: Yes.

Director: And your list can help you with this, can tell you when something's not right.

Handsome: That's right.

Director: So if you go on a date, and you feel a spark, but nothing gets checked....

Handsome: I'm probably wasting my time.

Director: Yes. But now do you know about the opposite problem?

Handsome: The opposite?

Director: Turning the wrong spark away.

Handsome: How would I do that?

Director: Well, I hate to say it — but you might be prejudiced.

Handsome: Prejudiced? And here we were just talking about having an open mind. So tell me. If I'm prejudiced, and the spark comes along — how will I perceive it?

Director: If it comes from a source you're prejudiced against? In all likelihood? You'll perceive it as a threat.

Handsome: The spark as a threat?

Director: Oh yes.

Handsome: So what should I do?

Director: All I can say is, be open to that spark, the right spark, from wherever it comes. If you are, you might well find your flame.

124. WORTH IT

Handsome: I'll be open to it, Director. And if I feel it as a threat, well, I'll just have to be brave.

Director: Yes. But fighting prejudice can be very hard, you know.

Handsome: The fight is worth it when love is at stake.

Director: I couldn't agree more. But what would you say to those who think love isn't worth the trouble?

Handsome: Not worth the trouble? I'd tell them they're fools.

Director: But what if they point out that love causes pain?

Handsome: True love never causes pain.

Director: Not even if you have to fight the hard fight against prejudice?

Handsome: It's not the love that causes pain in that case. It's the prejudice.

Director: A good reply. But what if they point out that there are misunderstandings in love, and these misunderstandings cause great pain?

Handsome: Well, of course. We're all human. But we work these things through. Look. People who don't believe in love will always point out this and that problem with love. I can only feel sorry for them for not knowing what they're missing.

Director: Is there anything we can do to persuade them to our point of view?

Handsome: We can find our loves and be the best possible examples of our truth.

Director: I like that. But it will be very hard to convince them. After all, is there any difference more fundamental than that between those who believe in love and those who don't?

Handsome: No, there isn't. And that's the honest truth.

Director: Yes. So do I even need to ask?

Handsome: Ask what?

Director: What kind of people do you want your friends to be?

Handsome: The kind that believes in love.

Director: And who do you value most in your family?

Handsome: Those who believe in love.

Director: And who are you going to love romantically?

Handsome: Someone who believes, with all her heart and soul, in love.

125. BELIEVING IN LOVE

Director: What does it mean to believe in love?

Handsome: I guess we can say that to believe in love means to value love.

Director: So to believe in love both heart and soul means to value love most highly?

Handsome: Yes.

Director: What's the value of love to those who value it most highly? Can you put it in words?

Handsome: Love makes life worth living. That's its value.

Director: There's no point to life without love?

Handsome: What sort of a life would it be?

Director: I suppose we could ask those who don't believe in love.

Handsome: Why bother? They won't have anything good to say.

Director: So we should only talk about love with those who believe in love?

Handsome: Well, there are those who come from loveless backgrounds who might want to talk to us, as we said before.

Director: Yes, they might become converts of sorts. And wouldn't they have that convert zeal?

Handsome: What do you mean?

Director: I mean, if they find love, won't they hold it all that much more precious as something they've never had?

Handsome: Yes, I think that's true.

Director: And isn't that a good example for those of us who come from love filled backgrounds?

Handsome: You mean there's a danger that we might take love for granted? Then yes, I think the converts make excellent examples for us to follow.

Director: Because they truly believe in love?

Handsome: Yes. They truly believe in love.

126. UNDERSTANDING

Director: Now, when two lovers believe together in love, what do they have?

Handsome: They have an understanding.

Director: Is that understanding based on belief, or is it based on something else?

Handsome: I'm not sure what you're getting at.

Director: I just mean, don't the lovers have to experience love first before they can believe and have their understanding?

Handsome: Of course they do.

Director: But when you experience love, wouldn't you say you know love?

Handsome: I would.

Director: So which comes first? Believing or knowing? Or don't you think there's any difference between the two?

Handsome: No, I think there's a difference. So here's how I think it goes. First you experience love, then you know it, and then you believe in it.

Director: And that's because we're saying to believe means to value.

Handsome: Right.

Director: But that's not what 'believe' always means, is it? I mean, typically we believe in things we don't know. For instance, I believe you'll write a summary of our conversation, but I don't know you will. Do you see what I'm getting at?

Handsome: Yes, of course.

Director: So, along these lines, lovers might know they have love or they might only believe they have love. But they don't know first and then believe. Am I making sense?

Handsome: You are.

Director: Now here's what's odd. You can value knowledge, right?

Handsome: Right.

Director: But can you value belief?

Handsome: You no doubt can.

Director: Can you value knowledge more than belief?

Handsome: Certainly.

Director: Then here's the final question. Can you value belief more than knowledge?

Handsome: We're still talking about love?

Director: We are. What do you think?

Handsome: Well, here's how I see it. You might believe in a love, believe in it very much. But you might also know, at some level, that the love isn't true. Your belief and your knowledge are at odds. So you have to make a choice. And some people choose to go on in their belief.

Director: In such a case, between two supposed lovers who both choose to believe against what they know, can there be an understanding?

Handsome: Yes, but not a good understanding.

Director: Why not?

Handsome: Because what sort of understanding can they have? An understanding that they're going to pretend they have pure and true love even though they don't?

Director: Yes, that's a problem.

Handsome: Of course it is.

Director: But lovers who value the love they know they have, can they have a good understanding?

Handsome: Certainly.

Director: Then is that what you want with your mate?

Handsome: It is. And that makes for an excellent, if obvious, item for the list.

127. THE LISTS

Director: I wonder, Handsome. Can the list serve more than one purpose?

Handsome: What do you mean?

Director: I mean, what about applying it to family and friends?

Handsome: Sure, I suppose we could do that. We could make a duplicate of the list for each, with some slight modifications. But with family it's a bit hard.

Director: How so?

Handsome: Suppose my list has seven items. And suppose a family member only scores two. Do I disown the person? Refuse to ever see her or him again?

Director: Yes, it's hard with family. But the important thing is what you know in your heart. You know you disagree on at least five important things. And you don't just have a vague sense of disagreement. You can name exactly where you differ. Don't you think it's good to have that clear a view?

Handsome: Yes, I do.

Director: And how is it with friends?

Handsome: It's the same. But if a friend only scores two on my list for friends, I have to wonder why we're friends.

Director: You might disown your friend? Refuse to see her or him again?

Handsome: I know it sounds terrible, but yes.

Director: So it's important that the list for friends be well made.

Handsome: It's important that all the lists be well made.

Director: Yes. And won't you, as you go on using the lists, learn? And when you've learned, might you not revise the lists to make them better?

Handsome: Of course.

Director: And one way to do this might be to retain the seven basic items, but to develop sub-items?

Handsome: You mean, item one might have ten sub-items? And if someone scores a five or six on the sub-items, I have to decide whether he or she gets to score a point on the top level item?

Director: Yes, it can get rather involved. So what do you think? Is more detail better? Will it help you come to a truer answer? Or will it be too much detail, clouding the view?

Handsome: I think we should have the detail. But if it goes against what we feel in our gut, we should ignore it.

128. Lies and Untruths

Director: Will your gut always be right?

Handsome: I like to think it will.

Director: But it's possible you'll be fooled?

Handsome: Of course, it's always possible to be fooled.

Director: And isn't this how it's done? The person in question tells you what you want to hear, and then lives the lie?

Handsome: Yes.

Director: But what if you sniff the lie out?

Handsome: That's easy. I break things off.

Director: But what if things are complicated?

Handsome: How so?

Director: Suppose you have an old friend, a friend from the time before the checklist. You decide to run through the questions with him. And you feel pretty sure he isn't being truthful on question four of seven. What do you do?

Handsome: Nothing.

Director: Nothing?

Handsome: Nothing at once. I gradually distance myself from him.

Director: Even if he's in agreement with you on all the other questions, honestly in agreement?

Handsome: If he disagreed on two questions, honestly so, we could still be friends. Maybe even three questions. But to lie to me? That I can't stand.

Director: But what if he wasn't lying?

Handsome: What do you mean?

Director: What if he just didn't know the true answer to your question?

Handsome: Why wouldn't he?

Director: Because it's a question about himself — and he doesn't know himself very well.

Handsome: I want friends who know themselves.

Director: Yes, but can't you help him come to know?

Handsome: What can I do? Tell him, Look, you don't know yourself?

Director: Why not?

Handsome: Because then what do I do if he asks me to tell him who or what he is?

Director: You tell him, if you know.

Handsome: And if I don't know?

Director: You tell him you don't know and offer to help.

Handsome: I think even if I know, I tell him I don't.

Director: Why?

Handsome: It's too shocking to hear who you are from another.

Director: But can't you lead him to the truth gradually?

Handsome: Yes. But in the end, he has to figure it out himself.

129. Bonds

Director: So where does love play in all of this? Do you love this person?

Handsome: Well, if I didn't why would I take the trouble to lead him to the truth?

Director: You love him because of his other answers to your questions?

Handsome: It's not his answers that make me love him.

Director: Are you going to tell me there has to be a spark as in romantic love?

Handsome: It's not quite a spark. It's something else. And I don't know if I'd call it an attraction either.

Director: Could it be a bond?

Handsome Yes, I think it could.

Director: A bond of trust and understanding?

Handsome: That sounds right.

Director: Now let's suppose your old friend out and out lies to you on question four, and you know it. Would this break the bond?

Handsome: Yes.

Director: Is that because you couldn't trust him anymore?

Handsome: It is.

Director: And without trust there can be no love?

Handsome: No good kind of love.

Director: And what about understanding? Can you have love if you don't have that?

Handsome: No, you can't have love without understanding.

Director: Now, I can see how a lie might well affect trust. But how would a lie affect understanding?

Handsome: It's simple, Director. I can't understand why my friend would lie to me.

Director: And so the lie opens a sort of gulf in the understanding between you and your friend? Is that it?

Handsome: Yes, exactly.

Director: But still, is there some understanding that remains? Or is it all gone with the lie?

Handsome: Well, I have to admit — some of it remains. But it's tainted.

Director: Can you maintain a bond with no trust and a tainted understanding?

Handsome: I don't see why you would.

Director: What if there's some trust just as there's some understanding? Is a bond possible?

Handsome: It's possible. But it won't be very good.

130. PURITY, FOUNDATION

Director: I wonder if there's a way out of all this.

Handsome: You mean a way toward forming a good bond once more?

Director: Yes. I mean, what if you come to see why your friend lied? Would that purify the understanding?

Handsome: Well, it might if he explained himself and offered an apology.

Director: Offering the apology is easy. Explaining himself is hard. Wouldn't you agree?

Handsome: Yes, I think that's true.

Director: If he says, I lied because I wanted so badly to keep the love of our friendship alive — what would you say to him?

Handsome: I'd say he didn't know me very well if he thought one differing view would be enough to end the friendship.

Director: And what if he says, But I wasn't confident enough to believe that?

Handsome: I'd say he should have tried to get to know me better before doubting me.

Director: So we're on to something interesting, Handsome. At first we were saying your friend has to get to know himself. But now we're saying he has to get to know you.

Handsome: Of course he has to get to know me, just as I'm trying to get to know him. There is no love in friendship if the two friends don't know each other.

Director: Where does the duty fall?

Handsome: What do you mean?

Director: I mean, does the duty fall solely on the friend trying to get to know the other friend? Or does the other friend have a duty to make himself known?

Handsome: Oh, I think he definitely has a duty to make himself known.

Director: And if each does this, tries to know the other and makes himself known, does that make for a sort of reciprocation?

Handsome: Certainly.

Director: And we were talking about reciprocation as the ideal in love, weren't we?

Handsome: We were.

Director: So if friends try to know one another and be known reciprocally, doesn't this make for a sort of purity in the relationship? Or is purity too strong a word?

Handsome: No, there's a purity that comes from knowledge.

Director: And from knowledge, love?

Handsome: Definitely — assuming, of course, that what they come to know is good.

Director: Now, we all know no one is perfectly good. Does one bit of something less than good ruin the love between friends?

Handsome: Of course not. What counts, above all else, is knowing that your friend is fundamentally good.

Director: And the root of your love for your friend takes hold right in this fundamental?

Handsome: Yes.

Director: Do the questions on your checklist try to get at the fundamental, or are they focused on more superficial things?

Handsome: No, they should try to get at the fundamental.

Director: Then let me ask you this. The fundamental — were we right to assume it's below the surface, as when we said it's where the root of our love takes hold?

Handsome: I think we were.

Director: Well, what if we were to describe it as the below ground foundation of a house?

Handsome: I think that's fine.

Director: But the foundation isn't all there is to a house.

Handsome: No, there's a lot more to a house.

Director: So how is it with friends? We agree there's a foundation to people, right?

Handsome: We agree.

Director: But then is there, as with a house, a lot more to people than the foundation?

Handsome: Of course.

Director: So here's what I'm wondering. If you have a friend who is strong beneath, but is falling apart above — do you want to stay friends?

Handsome: Yes, I do.

Director: Would you try to help him fix what's falling apart?

Handsome: I would.

Director: But what if it turns out you can't be much help? There's too much to fix. And, in fact, much of what's broken you don't know how to fix.

Handsome: Then I will just have to do the best that I can, and try to find friends or others who know what to do.

131. Falling Apart

Director: Now, let's switch from the love of friends back to romantic love. Do you think it's possible for you to love someone with a sound foundation but with everything above the surface falling apart, love that person romantically?

Handsome: If there's a flame? Yes, of course.

Director: Is there anything different about the lover we're describing and the friend we just described? I mean, aren't they fundamentally the same? Strong foundation and weak everything else?

Handsome: True.

Director: So what can you do for her?

Handsome: The same that I can do for my friend.

Director: You do your best and then bring in friends or others to help?

Handsome: Well, I'm not sure I'd bring them in — at least not for a while.

Director: Why not?

Handsome: You're going to think I'm bad.

Director: Why? Tell me.

Handsome: Doing my best... might take some time.

Director: I think I see what this is about. You want to keep her all to yourself!

132. FRIENDS

Handsome: Can you blame me? But there could be another reason, you know. What if she resists any help but mine because she's embarrassed?

Director: She only wants you to know about her plight?

Handsome: Yes.

Director: But if her house is truly falling apart, I have no doubt that you won't be the only one to see what's happening.

Handsome: True enough. But we're taking the extreme case. Let's say the house is more or less structurally sound. So there's no crisis.

Director: And no need to bring in help?

Handsome: No, no need. Can't I be the one to help her — alone?

Director: Ah, lovers. Always wanting to be alone.

Handsome: Well, what do you think?

Director: I think you should roll up your sleeves and get to work. There, now that you have my blessing are you ready to go out and find your fix-me-up love?

Handsome: I'm feeling pretty confident about finding my love, fix-me-up or not. But that's enough about romance. Let's talk a little more about friends.

Director: Well, you know what they say. A man with just one true friend should count himself lucky.

Handsome: Then I'm lucky. Because you're my true friend.

Director: And you are mine. Should we stop there?

Handsome: No. We need more friends.

Director: Why?

Handsome: So we can help each other out.

Director: Fixing up houses?

Handsome: Sure, fixing up houses. But also helping each other find The One.

Director: I thought we were done talking about romance.

Handsome: Friends need romance, too. And especially you!

Director: Well, you'll be pleased to know I went on a date just last week.

Handsome: With whom?

Director: Someone I met at the museum.

Handsome: Ha! How did it go?

Director: It was nice. We had lobster.

Handsome: No, I don't care what you had. What was it like with her?

Director: She's a wonderful conversationalist.

Handsome: What does she do?

Director: She teaches Italian at the university.

Handsome: What does she look like?

Director: I think she looks beautiful, though I'm not sure how good I'd be at describing why.

Handsome: What do you think she thought of you?

Director: I think she enjoyed our evening.

Handsome: Will you see her again?

Director: Yes, probably sometime in the museum.

Handsome: What? You'll just leave it to chance like that?

Director: She's not my One, Handsome.

Handsome: But how do you know?

Director: I just know. But look at the bright side.

Handsome: What bright side?

Director: I have a new friend.

133. The One?

Handsome: Will I get to meet this friend?

Director: Will I get to meet your lover?

Handsome: Of course you will — just as soon as I find her!

Director: Good. Then maybe the four of us could go out to dinner.

Handsome: But can't I meet your friend before then?

Director: Sure. But you'll have to come with me to the art gallery. And it might take several tries before we see her.

Handsome: Why don't you just call her and arrange a time?

Director: I like it better this way.

Handsome: You like relying on luck?

Director: Yes. It makes things exciting.

Handsome: But what's exciting? You already went out with her!

Director: What can I say, Handsome? I find it exciting not knowing what I'll find when I go to the museum. And you know what?

Handsome: What?

Director: I think she does, too. Why should I take that away from her?

Handsome: Why? Because you don't want her to be disappointed each time she goes to the museum and doesn't see you!

Director: Ah, but you don't know her like I do.

Handsome: What do you mean?

Director: She gets excited by the works of art. Sure, she might be wondering as she enters the museum whether she'll see me. But then she sees the beauty of the works before her. And she is transfixed. Sometimes I see her in that state and I just watch in wonder.

Handsome: You mean you don't even tell her you're there?

Director: Not for a few moments. Can you blame me?

Handsome: No, I suppose not. I'd like to see her when she's in that state. But I'd like to get to know her, too.

Director: Well then, we'll find the right time and I'll introduce you. But....

Handsome: But what?

Director: If I were unduly selfish, I might not want to do this.

Handsome: Why not?

Director: Because I think, Handsome.... I think she might be your One.

Handsome: What?

Director: Yes, she might be your One.

Handsome: I think you're teasing me.

Director: Why? You want a One, don't you?

Handsome: Of course I do!

Director: And you trust my ability to judge character?

Handsome: I trust you, definitely.

Director: And you trust my eye for beauty?

Handsome: Implicitly.

Director: And you trust my ability to judge, well, whatever else needs to be judged?

Handsome: You're the best judge of 'whatever else' I know.

Director: Then I think you may be in for a pleasant surprise. So long as....

Handsome: So long as what?

Director: So long as you're not in a great big rush.

Handsome: I can control myself. But why are you stressing this?

Director: Because she is, at heart, very shy.

Handsome: That would make me love her all the more!

Director: Look at you! You've heard ten words about her and now you're roaring for love!

Handsome: It's because I trust you, Director.

Director: I think it's less trust for me than cherished hopes for yourself!

Handsome: Well, there's some truth in that. So I should prepare myself.

Director: For what?

Handsome: Prepare myself to be let down.

Director: Who's going to let you down?

Handsome: I might let myself down.

Director: How?

Handsome: By being too nervous.

Director: A handsome, wealthy, powerful man being too nervous to meet a quietly beautiful teacher of a foreign tongue?

Handsome: Yes!

Director: What shall we do?

Handsome: What shall we do? What else can we do? But go forward.

134. A DEBT OF GRATITUDE

Director: Now, here's my concern. Am I going to lose two friends?

Handsome: What do you mean?

Director: Are you two going to disappear into blissful isolation?

Handsome: Well, that depends.

Director: Depends on whether she's really the One? Let's say she is. Am I going to lose you?

Handsome: No.

Director: Why?

Handsome: Because we'll owe you a debt of gratitude!

Director: And you think I'll enjoy your company knowing you're only with me because you feel obliged?

Handsome: You know that's not how it would be.

Director: Hmm. What if I could give you a way to pay your debt? Would you do it?

Handsome: Of course!

Director: And would you still remain my friends after the debt is paid?

Handsome: You know we would.

Director: But what I have in mind is a little dangerous.

Handsome: How so?

Director: You might fall and hurt yourself.

Handsome: What are you talking about?

Director: I want you to help me put a new roof on my house.

Handsome: Ha! That's really what you want?

Director: That's really what I want.

Handsome: And you're not speaking metaphorically?

Director: No, I have a very real leaky roof — and I need some help.

Handsome: If this works out, you've got it!

Director: Good. So, are you going to use the checklist on your potential love?

Handsome: Oh, the list! I suppose I should, don't you?

Director: Let me suggest this. Memorize it. Then walk through the questions casually, and not all at once, without seeming to attach much importance to them. Then, if you'd like, you and I can compare notes and see what we think.

Handsome: That sounds great. But our first time together will be the three of us?

Director: Well, if we see her at the gallery, we can ask her to stop out for a drink with us afterward. Would you prefer I not come?

Handsome: No! I mean, no. I'd rather you come. I want your opinion on whether you think the relationship can really work. But there's just one thing.

Director: What?

Handsome: What if she doesn't like me?

Director: Oh, I've asked about that.

Handsome: What? You told her about me?

Director: In all but glowing terms, yes.

Handsome: How did she... seem?

Director: Intrigued, and tried to hide it. That's a good sign, you know.

Handsome: Well, then I can't wait! But what if I don't like her?

Director: There's no harm in that at all. No promises have been made. There's just a bit of excitement in the air. It'll be a nice night out if nothing else comes of it. And isn't that how it should be?

Handsome: I agree.

Director: Good. She's usually at the gallery tomorrow night.

135. IN COMMON

Handsome: Maybe I should brush up on the masters.

Director: Why?

Handsome So I don't feel foolish when she knows more about them than I do.

Director: Oh, she doesn't know much about the masters.

Handsome: What does she know?

Director: She knows what she likes. She couldn't tell you what school, what technique, or whatever about the paintings she likes. She just knows she likes them.

Handsome: I'm liking her more and more.

Director: Yes, that's what I suspected.

Handsome: What else can you tell me about her?

Director: She has one very close friend on the faculty at the university and, as to everyone else there, she keeps to herself.

Handsome: I like that a great deal.

Director: More of her for you?

Handsome: Well... yes.

Director: Maybe she's looking for the same — more of you for her. Maybe it's on her checklist to find someone with lots of time to spend with her.

Handsome: Do you really think she keeps a checklist?

Director: We could ask her.

Handsome: No, let's not do that.

Director: Okay. But even if she doesn't have an actual list, can't we tell what it would be by the sorts of questions she asks?

Handsome: I suppose that's true. So she'll know what my list is based on what I ask, too.

Director: Of course. And that's one of the things she'll be weighing.

Handsome: What else will she be weighing?

Director: Your other likes and dislikes.

Handsome: You mean people, and events, and so on?

Director: Yes. And you'll be weighing the same.

Handsome: But it's a lot of pressure.

Director: What's the worst that happens?

Handsome: We find out that we have nothing in common.

Director: Do you think I would encourage the two of you to meet if I thought you had nothing in common?

Handsome: No, of course not.

Director: Then try to relax, Handsome. This time the odds are good.

Handsome: But there's still plenty that can go wrong.

Director: No doubt. But not as much as you think.

136. NORMAL, PHILOSOPHICAL

Handsome: But wait, now. Why did you talk to me about the dating service if you had this up your sleeve?

Director: There's no guarantee this will work. And it's good to have a backup plan.

Handsome: So tell me. Are we going to talk about our dialogues with the language instructor?

Director: Do you want to?

Handsome: Do you think she'll be interested?

Director: Well, she's a friend of mine. And she's interested in what she's heard about you. So I would assume she'd be interested in our dialogues.

Handsome: Okay. That makes sense. But what do we do? Re-enact them?

Director: Handsome. Do you really have such bad taste?

Handsome: Why are you being harsh?

Director: Because I want us to have a three-way dialogue with her!

Handsome: A real, live dialogue — on a date?

Director: Is it really a date with me there?

Handsome: Oh, of course — you have a point. But what will we talk about?

Director: What else? Love.

Handsome: Shouldn't that be a conversation I have with her alone?

Director: Why don't the three of us talk about love in general and then, if opportunity allows, you can have your private love talk with her about particulars later.

Handsome: That sounds good. But now I'm wondering. What would you say the difference is between the kind of dialogue the three of us will have and the kind of talk I'll have with her alone?

Director: Aside from the difference between the general and particulars? Well, the three of us will have a dialogue like the one we're having now. And I suppose we'd call such a dialogue philosophical, no?

Handsome: Yes.

Director: But you don't intend to be philosophical when you're alone with her, do you?

Handsome: No, I don't.

Director: How will you know you're not being philosophical?

Handsome: How will I know? It'll be obvious!

Director: How?

Handsome: I won't ask the kinds of questions we ask when we're being philosophical.

Director: What sort of questions will you ask?

Handsome: Normal questions.

Director: What's a normal question? Is it one you want the answer to?

Handsome: Of course.

Director: What about a philosophical question? Do you not want the answer to that?

Handsome: No, I want the answer.

Director: Then what's the difference?

Handsome: I know it when I see it.

Director: So tell me. Do you sometimes see this? A normal conversation becoming philosophical here and there, and a philosophical dialogue turning normal at points?

Handsome: Yes, I do.

Director: Well, now we have another excellent topic of conversation for when we get together with our friend from the museum.

Handsome: We're really going to talk to her about the difference between the normal and the philosophical and when the two blend?

Director: Yes, assuming she's interested.

Handsome: But here's a problem I see.

Director: Yes?

Handsome: What if we end up saying that for you, Director, the normal is the philosophical?

Director: And the normal for you, Handsome, is, well, normal? And we want to find out what her normal is?

Handsome: Don't you think we need to?

Director: Of course.

Handsome: But you already know, don't you?

Director: If I tend toward the philosophical side of things, and you tend toward the normal, with occasional outbreaks of dialogue like today, I'd say she's pretty well in the middle.

Handsome: Then maybe we shouldn't talk about what normal is for each of us.

Director: Why not?

Handsome: Because if she's that far along toward philosophy, she's not going to think very highly of me!

137. PHILOSOPHY

Director: Handsome, do you somehow believe that philosophical dialogue is better than normal conversation?

Handsome: Doesn't she?

Director: But that's not the point.

Handsome: I know. Look. Let me tell you why I suspect dialogue is best.

Director: Why?

Handsome: Because it helps you work things through.

Director: You can't do that in a normal conversation?

Handsome: You can, but it's not the same.

Director: Why not?

Handsome: Because you're not searching, truly searching for answers in a normal conversation.

Director: And that's what defines the philosophical — a search?

Handsome: Yes. Don't you agree?

Director: A search for the truth?

Handsome: Of course.

Director: What kind of truth? A truth for you, or a universal truth?

Handsome: A truth for you.

Director: You're not interested in universal truths?

Handsome: Of course I am. But I think what we're doing here today is more important than any search for universals.

Director: What are we doing?

Handsome: Helping me come to terms with love.

Director: And what about me? Where do I fit into all this?

Handsome: You're my guide.

Director: So I have nothing to learn?

Handsome: No, you learn. But you're learning about me. And some of what you learn about me you can use to learn about yourself.

Director: Let's assume what you're saying is true. Does this then mean that in a dialogue both parties always learn?

Handsome: Yes.

Director: And what about in regular conversation?

Handsome: Oh, you might learn something you didn't know, some news item, some gossip. But you don't often learn anything of fundamental importance.

Director: And philosophy always gets at the fundamental?

Handsome: It wouldn't be philosophy if it didn't.

Director: Are you worried about getting at the fundamental with our friend from the museum?

Handsome: Honestly? I am. I'm afraid I'm going to be embarrassed when I show how little I know.

Director: But isn't knowing when you don't know the first step toward philosophy? Don't you think she'll be impressed?

Handsome: Maybe. But now something occurs to me. You said she's halfway between philosophical and normal. But you didn't say whether she's sitting still or moving — and if moving, in which direction she's headed.

Director: An excellent point. She's moving. But is she moving toward philosophy or away from it? Let's ask her and see.

Handsome: Do you think it might be a little rude to ask something like that?

Director: No more rude than speaking of fundamental things.

Handsome: Then let's ask her where she's going.

138. Philosophy's House

Director: But, you know, this begs another question.

Handsome: What question?

Director: Are you, Handsome, moving toward or away from philosophy?

Handsome: I'm staying right where I am — in the doorway to normal with an eye on philosophy.

Director: Why not come over to the other side?

Handsome: Because I know myself better than that. Sure, I can have a talk with you like the one we're having today — and learn from it, and enjoy it. But on my own? I wouldn't know what to do. I think I would just stand there, confused.

Director: Until someone comes along and you start asking questions.

Handsome: But that's just it. I don't know what to ask. And even if I did, I don't have your thick skin. People don't usually respond well to questioning.

Director: You can develop a sense for the ones who do.

Handsome: But that's something that comes naturally to you. What comes naturally to me is something altogether different.

Director: What comes naturally to you? Love?

Handsome: Are you suggesting there's no love in philosophy?

Director: Why, no! There's the greatest love in philosophy.

Handsome: Don't tell me. The love of truth.

Director: No, I won't tell you that.

Handsome: Then what does philosophy love?

Director: Philosophers love human beings.

Handsome: In the sense that you love me as a friend?

Director: Yes.

Handsome: Do philosophers love romantically?

Director: You mean do they love their One? Some do. Some don't.

Handsome: Why wouldn't they?

Director: Maybe we can find some who don't and ask.

Handsome: I'll leave the talking to you. But I'm inclined to say that romantic love is a requirement for true philosophy.

Director: But if that's how it is, doesn't that entice you to step out of your doorway to normal and take a few steps toward philosophy?

Handsome: Honestly? I admit I'm intrigued.

Director: Well, leave a trail of bread crumbs behind you and head in the direction of philosophy's house. We can go together, if you'd like.

Handsome: Really? I thought you'd say philosophy is something you have to do on your own.

Director: Once you get into its house, yes. But on the way? There's every good reason to be with your friends.

Handsome: So what happens? You go in, you philosophize, and you come out a better person?

Director: Let's look at it this way, Handsome. What do you think the house of philosophy is a metaphor for?

Handsome: Your own mind.

Director: We all have to think on our own, don't we?

Handsome: There's no other way.

Director: And when we've thought, what do you think coming out again means?

Handsome: It means we share our thoughts with our friends.

Director: And when we learn things from them, what do you think we do?

Handsome: We go back in alone and think about what we've learned and see if it changes our way of looking at things.

Director: And so on?

Handsome: And so on.

Director: Now here's the thing. Once you start doing this there's no turning back. You must think on your own and then share your thoughts, and so on — all your life.

Handsome: And that's it?

Director: There's a bit more to it than that, which we can get to another time — but that's the basic story.

Handsome: I can do that.

Director: I thought you could.

Handsome: In fact, anyone could do that!

Director: If that's true, then why does philosophy's house seem empty more often than not?

139. WALKING AWAY

Handsome: I don't know, Director. But here's something I'm wondering. The woman from the museum. I asked if she's walking toward or away from philosophy.

Director: You did, and I thought it was an excellent question.

Handsome: Is it possible for someone who's walking toward philosophy to love someone who got close to philosophy but then turned around and walked away?

Director: A good question. But we should also ask if someone who is walking away from philosophy can love someone who's walking toward philosophy.

Handsome: Well, what do you think?

Director: I think it's possible for the one walking toward to love the one walking away. But I think it's very unlikely for the one walking away to love the one walking toward.

Handsome: Why?

Director: People can get funny, strange, when it comes to philosophy. Sometimes they walk away just as they get started. And when they do, they don't want to be reminded of it.

Handsome: But we're just talking about thinking and sharing our thoughts, right?

Director: Right. But sometimes as people start to think they sense a conclusion that frightens them.

Handsome: And so they go away and refuse to talk about it?

Director: Yes. Does that make sense to you?

Handsome: It does. So we have to be brave. And wouldn't it be good to have a mate who shares our courage? I'm going to have to modify my list.

140. A Mind of Your Own

Director: So you're looking for a love with philosophical courage.

Handsome: I am. But what about you?

Director: Me? Someone like that would be just the thing. But tell me. What do you get when you have courage concerning thought?

Handsome: I'm not sure.

Director: Don't you come to develop — a mind of your own?

Handsome: Yes, of course.

Director: And you want a mate with a mind of her own.

Handsome: I do. Does the woman from the museum have one?

Director: From what I can tell so far? Yes, I think she does.

Handsome: Then I'm in luck! But do you know what I think? I think we should see if we can find a fourth to join us for dinner with the woman from the museum!

Director: You mean someone for me.

Handsome: Yes!

Director: If I find one, I'll be sure to invite her.

Handsome: And I'll do the same!

Director: Oh, but be careful, Handsome.

Handsome: What? You don't trust my judgment?

Director: I'm afraid you might confuse being opinionated with having a mind of your own.

Handsome: Come on! Of course I know the difference between those two types of mind.

Director: What's the difference?

Handsome: Opinionated minds are hard. Minds of their own are supple, though they can get firm.

Director: Well, you're giving me some confidence. So it'll be the four of us, walking together toward the house of philosophy, lingering along the way to share our thoughts, questioning when we don't understand. And when the time comes to say goodnight, each of us will retire into her or his own mind, reviewing all that was said, and thinking things through. How does that sound to you?

Handsome: That sounds very good. But....

Director: Yes?

Handsome: I wonder if... I'll ever get... jealous.

Director: Jealous of what?

Handsome: Her having a mind of her own.

Director: You need to have a mind of your own in order not to get jealous of the mind of another.

Handsome: That's the thing. I'm not sure how much of a mind of my own I have, to tell you the truth.

Director: It's not always an easy thing to have. But remember — if you practice philosophy, the mind you want, the mind you're looking for, will take shape.

Handsome: But what if the woman from the museum's mind takes shape faster than mine?

Director: This isn't a race, Handsome. We have no choice but to go at our own pace — no good choice, at any rate. Focus on developing your own mind, not on chasing after someone else.

Handsome: But how can she think I'm her One if I'm not ready for her with a mind of my own?

Director: She might see that you've come a long way, and might very well like the direction you're headed.

141. DOMINATION

Handsome: That would be wonderful. But, you know, I don't think everyone sees it the way we see it.

Director: How do they see it?

Handsome: They think their Ones shouldn't have minds of their own.

Director: Why do you think that is?

Handsome: I think they want to control their Ones' minds.

Director: Why would someone want to control someone else's mind?

Handsome: I know, it's an alien concept, right? I don't know why. But I think it happens all the time.

Director: Is one mind always dominant and the other submissive, or can they take turns dominating one another?

Handsome: Oh, I think they can definitely take turns. And believe it or not, I think they think this means they're in a healthy, give-and-take relationship.

Director: But why dominate?

Handsome: I guess it covers up insecurities.

Director: And why allow yourself to be dominated?

Handsome: Because you have very bad insecurities.

Director: Does having insecurities make you a bad person?

Handsome: No, of course not.

Director: What can you do to get rid of your insecurities?

Handsome: You can try to find a One that soothes them and helps you develop a mind of your own.

142. Born To Be

Director: Don't you think that's what every One should do — help develop and soothe?

Handsome: I do. But then that makes me wonder. Do Ones just naturally know how to be Ones? Or do they need to learn how?

Director: Which would you prefer?

Handsome: I'd prefer that they learn how — because I don't yet feel that I'm a One!

Director: Then let's say you were born to be a One and are just in the process of becoming fully yourself.

Handsome: But is everyone born to be a One?

Director: I don't know. Maybe.

Handsome: Maybe? That's all you have to say?

Director: Well, we could say that those who fail to become Ones were never meant to be Ones. They weren't born to be Ones.

Handsome: But that's saying nothing. We could also say that they were meant to be Ones but awful circumstances got in the way.

Director: Yes, we could say that. And we could also say they didn't try very hard. I think we could have a long discussion about this. But let's say everyone is meant to be a One. And let's say there are two aspects to this — what you yourself do to become a One, and how circumstances factor in. So what do you need to do?

Handsome: You need to train your mind to be your own. After all, how can you help another to have a mind of their own if you don't have a mind of your own?

Director: A good point. And how do you train your mind for that?

Handsome: You rely on what you yourself think and not what others tell you to think.

Director: Okay. What else?

Handsome: You have to know how to soothe insecurities.

Director: How do you know how to do that?

Handsome: I'm not sure.

Director: Maybe you learn from someone who knows how?

Handsome: Yes, maybe. Or maybe you teach yourself by means of trial and error as you go?

Director: Yes, and maybe it's a bit of both. So what else do we need to know?

Handsome: I think that's it.

Director: Good. Now we should talk about circumstances. And here's something I don't understand. How can circumstances possibly get in the way of your thinking for yourself? I mean, even in the worst of circumstances, can't you think on your own?

Handsome: People are afraid to. What can I say?

Director: But what are they afraid of?

Handsome: I think they're afraid they'll think differently than others.

Director: And, what, these others will punish them for doing so?

Handsome: More or less, in one form or another — yes.

Director: So they'd rather not become a One.

Handsome: I don't think they consciously make that choice. I think it just happens.

Director: Because circumstances, the thoughts of others, are overwhelming?

Handsome: Yes.

Director: Well, this, too, could make for an excellent topic of conversation for our dinner. The brave souls who overcome the pressure of the thought of others in order to become what they're meant to be — and those who fail.

Handsome: But do you think that might be too heavy a topic? And what if our dates believe there's someone, a One, for everyone — even those who fail?

Director: I don't think it's too heavy a topic. And if they think you don't have to be a One to have a One, we'll just have to ask them why.

143. PLANNING

Handsome: I'm afraid it's going to turn into an argument.

Director: If we keep it lighthearted, I bet we'll be alright.

Handsome: Are you worried that I'll be too serious?

Director: Oh, I'm not worried about you in particular. Any one of us might grow too serious.

Handsome: It's not very philosophical to grow too serious, is it?

Director: Are you suggesting philosophy isn't a serious business?

Handsome: Is it?

Director: It's serious enough. So how will we open our conversation?

Handsome: You want to plan it all out ahead?

Director: Well, you know what they say about plans for war — they're useless after the first shot is fired.

Handsome: Then why bother to plan at all?

Director: It's a pleasant way to spend our time. And that first shot is important.

Handsome: Okay. We could just throw it out there and ask: Do you believe there's someone for everyone?

Director: But should we really start with a question about love? I mean, true love follows from being a One. Right? So shouldn't we begin with a question concerning being a One?

Handsome: A good point. So we'll ask: Do you think everyone can have a mind of their own?

Director: I think that's a better place to start. Then we can ease our way gradually into the topic of love.

Handsome: So maybe after we talk about minds of our own for a while, we ask: What role does having a mind of your own play when it comes to love?

Director: Ah, that's a good question. The conversation should open right up at this point — provided you did your job.

Handsome: What job?

Director: Finding me just the right date!

Handsome: I'll do the best I can! But somehow I think you know how to handle yourself well even under adverse conditions.

Director: I'd prefer to do so under favorable conditions.

Handsome: Then why not pick someone out for yourself?

Director: And ruin the surprise? When you've been looking for as long as I have, Handsome, you appreciate the play of luck and the charm of the unknown.

Handsome: Alright. It's up to me, then. But don't think I didn't notice that you equate my efforts with the play of luck.

144. MORE THAN LUCK

Director: Will you use your checklist for me?

Handsome: Now you're going to mock my checklist?

Director: I just want to know how you'll go about finding my date.

Handsome: I'll use the checklist. But if she makes me simmer — you're out of luck!

Director: Let me ask you a terrible question, Handsome.

Handsome: Oh boy. What?

Director: What if she makes both of us simmer?

Handsome: Then I suppose dinner will be even more interesting!

Director: But if you and I are simmering for my date, what do we do about your date?

Handsome: Ha! I have no idea!

Director: Now let me ask you the next hard question.

Handsome: Go ahead.

Director: What if you're simmering for her, too?

Handsome: I'm simmering for both?

Director: Do you think it's even possible?

Handsome: Of course it is!

Director: What should you do?

Handsome: Get away as quickly as possible?

Director: What, just up and leave the table?

Handsome: Well, what else can I do?

Director: Change the topic of conversation.

Handsome: You think that will really do the trick?

Director: If it's something that will cool things down, yes.

Handsome: What can I say?

Director: Assuming we've been talking about romantic love, maybe you subtly redirect the conversation onto the topic of the love of friends.

Handsome: Yes, that's a beautiful topic. And it gets us off the romantic theme.

Director: So we'll say there's romantic love on the one hand, and brotherly or sisterly love on the other.

Handsome: Yes, and then we might point out that brothers can love sisters and sisters can love brothers — and what do you call it then? Sibling-ly love?

Director: Yes, and then you might escape into a discussion of nouns and the formation of adjectives.

Handsome: And that's how I'll cool my water?

Director: Nothing like a good conversation about nouns and adjectives to cool you down.

Handsome: Well, I can't think of anything better. But seriously now. Let's say I'm simmering only for my date. What do I do?

Director: Keep your water cool. Come closer and feel the simmer. Then back off and feel cool once again. Do you remember what we discussed along these lines?

Handsome: I remember.

Director: Then dare as much talk about romantic love as you can. I'll keep an eye on you to make sure you don't get too hot. And if we can avoid that, we'll get a better sense if she might truly be your One.

145. FLIRTING

Handsome: But there's just one thing.

Director: Oh?

Handsome: I know we touched on this before. But I can't help worrying, and I worry for both of us. If we keep on getting close then pulling away, won't they think there's something wrong?

Director: You mean either with them or with us?

Handsome: Yes, either.

Director: What could be wrong with us?

Handsome: We might be very shy. Or we might not know what we want. Or we're playing some game.

Director: And what might be wrong with them?

Handsome: I don't know. They might have insecurities and our actions feed them.

Director: Hmm. I see what you mean. So what can we do?

Handsome: Plant ourselves at a safe distance, outside of simmer range, and stay there until we learn what we need to know.

Director: And we need to know if these women are our Ones?

Handsome: Yes.

Director And we'll be able to know without a few good simmers? But let's forget about simmering and keeping our water cool and any other metaphor. If you come close to someone, make a few pleasant comments, then gently pull away — what are you doing?

Handsome: You're flirting.

Director: Do you see anything wrong with flirting?

Handsome: I don't see anything wrong with it. No one gets hurt if it's done right.

Director: The one you flirt with doesn't get hurt?

Handsome: If you keep things light? No.

Director: And what about you? Do you ever get hurt?

Handsome: Again, if you keep it light — no.

Director: What would it mean to be too heavy?

Handsome: To be too serious.

Director: Flirting should never be serious?

Handsome: Flirting can open the door to something serious, but it should never be serious in and of itself.

Director: Do you think people just somehow know this instinctively? That it's good to start light?

Handsome: People do seem to know this.

Director: Because they don't want anyone to get hurt?

Handsome: Yes, I think that's right — at least that's how it is among the better types of soul.

146. SERIOUS

Director: What about being serious can cause someone to get hurt?

Handsome: I think it has to do with expectations.

Director: What do you mean?

Handsome: You get your hopes up.

Director: And then your hopes are dashed?

Handsome: Yes.

Director: Whose fault is it your hopes got so high?

Handsome: It could be both people's fault.

Director: Yours because you were too serious in your hope?

Handsome: That's right.

Director: What exactly happens when you're too serious in your hope?

Handsome: You start to believe.

Director: Believe you've found your One?

Handsome: Right.

Director: But shouldn't you confirm that it's really your One?

Handsome: You should. But that's not always what happens.

Director: Why?

Handsome: Because sometimes it seems like you'll never find your One. And you get desperate.

Director: But if you're desperate isn't it more important than ever to confirm that it's really The One?

Handsome: Yes, that's true. And it's a terrible dilemma.

Director: What can we do to make it less terrible?

Handsome: I'm not sure we can do anything.

Director: Can't we just stop believing, enjoy some flirting, and see where it goes?

Handsome: But what if the other is misleading us?

Director: You mean what if the flirting isn't innocent?

Handsome: Yes. What then?

Director: We break things off.

Handsome: So we have to find a way to tell if flirting is innocent or not. But if we're desperate, how can we find that way?

Director: I think we have to start with a healthy dose of self-respect.

Handsome: I agree. So let's say we can tell that the flirting is innocent. That's fine. But what if it goes nowhere?

Director: Well, let me ask. Is flirting unpleasant?

Handsome: Always? No, of course not. Flirting can be pleasant. But sometimes it's unpleasant for the one being flirted with.

Director: Assuming it's of the pleasant variety, what's wrong with a little flirting that goes nowhere? In other words, what's wrong with flirting with someone who's not your One?

Handsome: The problem is that your One might come along while you're distracted by the flirting. And besides, to flirt like that just seems shallow.

Director: Shallow? You'd rather get down into the depths of seriousness when you flirt?

Handsome: I'd rather not have to flirt at all. I'd rather have my One and be as serious with her as I like.

Director: Yes, but how serious should you be?

Handsome: What do you mean?

Director: Will you be serious all of the time?

Handsome: No, of course not.

Director: Why not?

Handsome: Because some things you have to take lightly.

Director: And some things seriously? And if you take the serious things lightly and the light things seriously?

Handsome: You're in danger of losing your One.

147. Weight

Director: So it's important to know the difference between serious and light.

Handsome: It's vital.

Director: Then how do we know?

Handsome: We just know.

Director: Do we know by weight?

Handsome: You mean like weighing on your chest or shoulders?

Director: Yes. How much do you think a serious thing weighs?

Handsome: Too much.

Director: Okay. And how much does a light thing weigh?

Handsome: I don't think we should say it weighs anything. In fact, I think we should say it takes away weight. But there's a problem.

Director: Oh?

Handsome: What if something that seems light to my One weighs heavily on me?

Director: I suppose you have to take it seriously.

Handsome: I agree. But won't this make for trouble? One of us feeling one thing and the other something else?

Director: It depends on how you handle the situation. But you said something interesting. You said a light thing takes away weight. What if your partner can offer you something light, something light enough to take all the weight off of your shoulders, at least for a while? Do you take it?

Handsome: Of course I do. But what could she possibly offer me to do that?

Director: Why, the lightest of all light things — a laugh.

148. LAUGHTER

Handsome: But what if the burden I'm carrying is so great that I can't laugh?

Director: You can never laugh? Then you probably haven't found true love.

Handsome: Laughter is that important?

Director: Of course it is! Don't you think you should laugh more freely and more often with no one but your love? Good natural laughs. Spontaneous laughs. Not phony conversational laughs.

Handsome: What is it about love that makes for laughter?

Director: What is it about anything that makes for laughter?

Handsome: I've heard it said that we laugh when an unexpected truth comes out.

Director: Really? Well, I suppose that applies to lovers. Each should be a treasure trove of truths to the other. And when one pops out suddenly? We laugh.

Handsome: Yes. But what else can laughter do besides take weight off our shoulders?

Director: Have you ever noticed that with lovers there's an affectionate afterglow to a good laugh?

Handsome: I have.

Director: That afterglow is the bond between the lovers sealing tight.

Handsome: I see. But, and I hope you don't take this the wrong way — how tight do we want it?

Director: Yes, I know what you mean. We need to be able to breathe.

Handsome: So what do we do?

Director: This might seem too neat a thing, but we laugh.

Handsome: And what does that do?

Director: When we laugh the seal breaks and fresh air comes in, before the bond seals up again.

Handsome: So no laughter, no seal? And no laughter, no air?

Director: That's how it seems to me. Isn't that how it seems to you?

149. Air

Handsome: Yes, it does seem that way to me. But I need to get clear on something. What is 'air' in our metaphor?

Director: Freshness.

Handsome: But what is 'freshness'?

Director: The opposite of that stale feeling many couples experience.

Handsome: What gets stale?

Director: For one? Their conversation.

Handsome: Do they have nothing to talk about?

Director: Yes, I think that's true for many. And some just talk for the sake of talking, but without any fresh air.

Handsome: So eventually they feel like they're suffocating.

Director: Precisely.

Handsome: They need a good laugh.

Director: Desperately.

Handsome: And if they can't laugh?

Director: They might lack true love.

Handsome: But what if they don't lack true love?

Director: Then they need to see that fresh air is more than fresh air.

Handsome: I don't understand.

Director: Fresh air is interest, my friend.

Handsome: Interest?

Director: Yes, as in taking an interest in life.

Handsome: What makes you take an interest in life?

Director: I think you should tell me.

Handsome: Alright. It's love. Love makes you take an interest in life. So you're saying these couples need more love?

Director: Don't you think that's true?

Handsome: I do. But that means the flame of true love can burn brighter and dimmer at times?

Director: Yes. And what's worse — it can even go out.

150. REKINDLING

Handsome: I don't like to think that.

Director: Neither do I. But don't you think we should be prepared?

Handsome: Yes. So how can we rekindle the flame?

Director: I know of a way. But I don't think you'll believe me.

Handsome: Try me.

Director: We can rekindle our flame through comedy.

Handsome: Comedy? That's what you think will work?

Director: Yes. But it's comedy taken in the lightest and gentlest sense. We have to find ways to make each other smile.

Handsome: And you think smiles are enough to revive love?

Director: Don't you think they're at least a good start?

Handsome: Well yes, I do. But I'll tell you a better place to begin.

Director: Where?

Handsome: With reaffirmation of mutual trust and admiration. You can't have love without those two things.

Director: Yes, I see what you mean. But tell me, Handsome. Would you trust someone who has absolutely no sense of humor?

Handsome: Not in the least? No, I don't suppose I would. There's something wrong there.

Director: Yes. And what about admiration? Would you admire someone devoid of humor?

Handsome: No, I wouldn't admire someone like that.

Director: So if you can't have love without trust and admiration, and you can't have them without humor — then isn't the comic the foundation of love? And if that's true, then isn't it obvious what's truly the best place to start trying to rekindle the flame?

151. THE COMIC

Handsome: I feel like you're making sense. But I don't want to agree.

Director: Why?

Handsome: Because we seem to be making light of love.

Director: Because love should have a more serious foundation than comedy?

Handsome: Yes.

Director: Well, maybe this will help. What's more important than truth?

Handsome: Truth? I'm not sure anything is more important.

Director: Are you forgetting about love?

Handsome: Truth and love are equally important. You can't have love without truth. And maybe you can't have truth, the whole truth, without love, either.

Director: So love and truth go together. Now let's turn to the comic. What can we say about the comic?

Handsome: That it makes us laugh or smile.

Director: How does it do this?

Handsome: By bringing out unexpected truths.

Director: Is something that brings out truth important?

Handsome: Of course it is.

Director: If something is important should we take it seriously?

Handsome: We no doubt should. And I see where this is headed.

Director: Where?

Handsome: If we take comedy seriously, love's reliance on comedy in no way makes light of love.

Director: Yes. Do you believe it?

Handsome: I do.

Director: Good. Now give us an example of a rare and unexpected truth.

Handsome: Who, me? I can't think of anything offhand like that!

Director: Why not?

Handsome: Because I'm not a comedian!

Director: But you don't have to be a comedian to be funny.

Handsome: Yes, but I don't have a stock of ready-made comedy at hand.

Director: You're the spontaneous type?

Handsome: I am.

Director: Are you that way with both the lowest form of comedy and the highest?

Handsome: With both, yes. But what's the highest form of comedy?

Director: The comedy of love as told by a philosopher.

Handsome: Ha! And why do you think that is?

Director: Because it's a universal theme articulated by someone who knows.

Handsome: And just what do philosophers know?

Director: Would you agree that love involves sweet nothings?

Handsome: I would, yes. But they really are something, you know.

Director: That's what philosophers know.

Handsome: What do you mean?

Director: They know nothing can be something, and something can be nothing.

Handsome: But what are you saying? Do you think love is nothing?

Director: Oh no, to the contrary! Love is most definitely something, a very big and great something! But there's a lot of nothing in what many people take as the something of love. Just as true lovers can have something in what others might take as nothing. The confusion about this is where the comedy lies.

Handsome: But why is it comedy and not tragedy if people are confused when it comes to love?

Director: Why? Because it's just too sad to think of it in any other way.

152. THE TRAGIC

Handsome: Tell me, Director. Can a philosopher render a comic account of tragedy itself?

Director: I think it's possible. But shouldn't we concern ourselves first with knowing what tragedy is before we trouble ourselves with the kind of account we can give?

Handsome: Yes. So what is tragedy, oh philosopher?

Director: As concerns love? Thinking you have love when you don't.

Handsome: That's it? That's all you have to say?

Director: Do you want the truth or some story?

Handsome: The truth! But it can't be that simple.

Director: Why not?

Handsome: Because then every pair of infatuated youths is tragic in its own way!

Director: You mean it's not?

Handsome: Alright. I'll agree. But if it really is so simple then tell me what philosophers can do for the tragic in love.

Director: They can find a way to bring air to them or them to air — and get them to breathe.

Handsome: But there's a problem with all tragic love. The bond, the seal that we talked about, even if it's only on one side — it can be very, very strong. Air never gets in.

Director: Not even with a great big laugh?

Handsome: The tragic really aren't given to laughter, at least not healthy laughter, as I think you know.

Director: So what do you think we can do?

Handsome: Maybe you can reason with them.

Director: Reason can break a seal and let in air?

Handsome: I think it can — if the reasons are strong.

Director: How's this for a reason? You're suffocating and if you don't break free you'll die.

Handsome: That's a pretty powerful reason.

Director: But will it work?

Handsome: It depends on the reasoner.

Director: On the reasoner? How?

Handsome: You have to establish trust and admiration.

Director: In other words, you have to become a friend?

Handsome: Yes.

Director: And once you're a friend, then someone might listen?

Handsome: Exactly. But then when they're listening you might have a chance at introducing a breath of comedy. And that might do the trick.

Director: You mean that might keep them alive.

Handsome: Right. And isn't that what the other part of philosophy is, the part you said we could get to another time?

Director: Making friends and making sure that they don't die?

Handsome: Yes.

Director: But do we make friends all for the sake of a rescue? Or do we make friends for the sake of the good things that come from being friends?

Handsome: Why can't it be both?

Director: I suppose you have a point. So the answer to tragic love is philosophical friendship?

Handsome: Yes, I think it is.

153. STRONGER

Director: Tell me, Handsome. Are we saying that the love of friendship must be stronger than the tragic love in order for the tragic soul to be saved?

Handsome: Yes, we are.

Director: Are we also saying we know, absolutely know the tragic soul isn't with its One?

Handsome: By definition, yes. There's nothing tragic about being with your One.

Director: Ever?

Handsome: Never.

Director: Would it help if our tragic friends could believe that?

Handsome: Not 'believe', Director — know.

Director: How do we get them to know?

Handsome: I don't know.

Director: Do we have to find them their One? Is that the only proof that tragic souls would believe?

Handsome: In some cases, yes. And if we can't find their One, there's a danger.

Director: What danger?

Handsome: That the tragic souls might believe that you, or I, or whoever comes as a friend — they might believe that we're The One.

Director: Not good.

Handsome: No, not good at all.

Director: So no flirting.

Handsome: No, and no simmering.

Director: This is all strictly on a friendly basis.

Handsome: Yes.

Director: But a basis strong enough to convince them to leave their tragic love.

154. AMBITION

Handsome: But sometimes with even the strongest footing we won't be able to convince them.

Director: What else can we do?

Handsome: There's something the tragic can do for themselves.

Director: Oh? What?

Handsome: They can turn to art.

Director: Art? Art succeeds where friendship fails?

Handsome: Well, it's not so much the art as it is the ambition to create.

Director: How will such ambition save these tragic souls?

Handsome: It will focus them.

Director: To the exclusion of their tragic love?

Handsome: Exactly.

Director: This must be a very powerful ambition.

Handsome: It's all consuming, at least at first.

Director: That sounds dangerous, my friend.

Handsome: That's why it's best expressed in art.

Director: What does it take to arrive at such an ambition?

Handsome: Well, here's the catch. It takes a dry soul.

Director: What do you mean?

Handsome: In order to explain I'm going to have to change our image of tragic love. Do you mind?

Director: Not at all.

Handsome: Okay. Here's how it goes. Tragic love is unhealthy love. Yes?

Director: Yes.

Handsome: Well, unhealthy love makes for a damp soul. Would you agree?

Director: I would.

Handsome: And when the soul is damp it's impossible for the spark of ambition to light the soul ablaze.

Director: No doubt. But now you've led us into a dilemma. I mean, we're saying the ambition does away with the tragic love. But we can't have the ambition until our soul gets dry enough to light. In other words, we can't have the ambition that gets rid of the tragic love without getting rid of the tragic love first! Are we calling for some sort of miracle? Or is there something more you're not telling me?

Handsome: I think I've told you enough. All I'll add is that it's not impossible to get out of the dilemma. Consider it a riddle. And know that it's been solved before.

Director: I'd like to talk to the one who solved it! But tell me. What sort of artist did this person become after the seemingly miraculous change?

Handsome: A healthy artist, if not a very good artist — and one more open to life.

155. MUSIC

Director: More open to life because tragedy closes you off from life?

Handsome: Yes.

Director: But isn't tragedy part of life?

Handsome: Well, yes. But it's best observed from without. But let's shift the conversation a bit.

Director: Where to?

Handsome: To something I've often wondered about. Do you think you can tell if someone is tragic at heart just by knowing what type of music they like?

Director: No, I don't think it's quite that simple. But I do think you can learn a lot about people based on their tastes.

Handsome: What sort of music do you like?

Director: Oh, a variety. But mostly I find myself coming back to the Baroque in general and Telemann in particular. How about you?

Handsome: Well, I have to admit — I have a taste for what you might call tragic music.

Director: Tragic music? What do you mean by that?

Handsome: You know, the melancholy — the sad, the mournful, and so on. Do you think my liking this sort of music means I'm inherently tragic?

Director: No, I wouldn't say that. But if you dwell on such music too much....

Handsome: What?

Director: Too much of that stuff might incline you toward a tragic point of view.

Handsome: Yes. But what about you?

Director: What about me?

Handsome: Won't too much of your music incline you toward... a pretentious point of view?

156. Pretension, Reason

Director: Well, we're talking about love. So when it comes to love, what's better? To be pretentious or tragic?

Handsome: You're taking me seriously?

Director: Sure. Why not?

Handsome: I was just kidding! I don't think you're pretentious. And you know that.

Director: Handsome, how do you know what I know? But let's do this. Regardless of how serious we are, why don't you answer the question and let's see where we go?

Handsome: Alright. When it comes to love I have to say it's better to be pretentious rather than tragic, despite the bad taste it leaves in my mouth.

Director: Why?

Handsome: Because I suppose you're healthier when you're pretentious than when you're tragic. And healthier people have healthier loves.

Director: Then let me ask you this. Whom do you think it's easier to reason with concerning matters of the heart? Is it someone who's pretentious?

Handsome: No, I think the pretentious are often deaf to reason.

Director: So it's easier to reason with the tragic?

Handsome: I don't know. They can be deaf, too.

Director: What does reason do when confronted with the deaf?

Handsome: Turn and run the other way?

Director: No, Handsome. It makes a final appeal.

Handsome: To what?

Director: Self-love.

Handsome: And what does this appeal to self-love amount to?

Director: Proof that you can't love yourself if you're not open to reason.

Handsome: That's a proof I'd like to hear!

Director: Fortunately, you don't need to. So let's say our pretentious and tragic friends come around and listen. What have we got?

Handsome: Friends who understand what makes reason so sweet?

Director: I'm inclined to agree. But I was thinking this. We probably still have one friend who tends to be pretentious and another who tends to be tragic. But each of them will be just a little bit less so than before. And isn't that much?

Handsome: Very much.

Director: So which will it be for you?

Handsome: What, you mean whether I want to tend to be tragic or pretentious? And I have to choose? Well, if I'm honest, I'd have to say, and I don't know why I feel this way, but I'd have to say I'd rather be tragic.

Director: And to play devil's advocate I'll say I'd rather be pretentious. But here's the thing. What about comedy?

Handsome: Well, it's obvious. You're the comic figure.

Director: Why, exactly?

Handsome: Because there's something ridiculous about all pretension. But I can see how pretension can be tragic, too.

Director: How?

Handsome: By being so wrapped up in itself that it's out of touch with its love.

Director: But what about the tragic? Are they ever comic?

Handsome: No, I don't see how we can say they are — despite what we said about a comic account of tragedy by philosophy.

Director: Then do we have to conclude that, overall, pretension is the better of the two? I mean, it's oftentimes comic, whereas we're saying the tragic isn't.

Handsome: To the extent we believe that comedy is better than tragedy? Yes. So I suppose you've shown good reason to love the music you love.

157. Love the Music

Director: But that's not why I love the music I love.

Handsome: Why do you love it?

Director: Because it speaks to me.

Handsome: That's why I love the music I love.

Director: What does it tell you?

Handsome: What does it tell me? It tells me.... It tells....

Director: Does it tell you to be graceful?

Handsome: Mostly.

Director: Does it tell you to feel composed?

Handsome: Yes... when it's not making me cry.

Director: Does it tell you to feel unity in complexity?

Handsome: I'm not sure.

Director: How about the gradual and gentle strengthening of themes? Does it tell you about that?

Handsome: I guess you could say it does. But is that really what your music says to you?

Director: Of course, and that's not all.

Handsome: I'd like to listen to some of that.

Director: Why, certainly. I'll get you some right away. But who would you rather love?

Handsome: Excuse me?

Director: Who would you rather love? Someone who embodies grace, and composure, and unified complexity, and the gradual strengthening of themes, and so much more — or someone else?

Handsome: That's the sort of person I would want to love, the former.

Director: Then I'd really better get you some of my music right away.

158. A Love Who Loves

Handsome: But now you're teasing me again.

Director: How so?

Handsome: You're making it sound as if music can make all the difference.

Director: Of course it can't make all the difference. But it can help.

Handsome: How?

Director: Music can train you.

Handsome: And tragic music trains you to cry?

Director: Well, I suppose there's a bit more to it than that. But yes.

Handsome: And what does your music train you for?

Director: All the things we said.

Handsome: Grace, and composure, and so on?

Director: Yes.

Handsome: Well, then I definitely want a love who loves your type of music.

Director: Without loving the music yourself?

Handsome: I intend to learn how.

Director: In the same way you might learn how to love someone who loves this type of music?

Handsome: I would just love her, Director. No learning required.

Director: So will you put this on your checklist? Must love good music?

Handsome: Why not?

Director: Because you don't really know that it's good music.

Handsome: But we just explained how it is!

Director: Right now you merely believe me that it's good music. You don't actually appreciate it yourself.

Handsome: True.

Director: And can't it be that way with a person?

Handsome: You mean I might believe someone is good for me without actually appreciating her for who she truly is? Yes, I think it can be that way.

Director: Then don't let it be that way with you.

159. APPRECIATION

Handsome: You're right to make that point. But now I'd like to talk some more about what it means to appreciate something.

Director: Don't we agree it means to recognize and enjoy worth?

Handsome: Full recognition and enjoyment?

Director: Ideally, yes.

Handsome: It takes time to appreciate something fully, doesn't it?

Director: It certainly can.

Handsome: Why do you say it 'can'?

Director: Because one person might walk right up and fully appreciate the thing in question at once. But someone else might need time to learn to appreciate it.

Handsome: Does that make the one person better than the other?

Director: Better at appreciating the thing in question.

Handsome: But once you learn to appreciate it, you'll immediately be able to recognize it and enjoy it the next time you see it?

Director: If it's truly the same thing and it isn't somehow obscured? Yes.

Handsome: Okay. But now let's focus on people.

Director: Alright.

Handsome: Once you come to appreciate certain people, it's obvious that any time you see them you'll be able to appreciate them again. Right?

Director: Right, unless they've changed.

Handsome: Of course. But what about other people, people who are a lot like the people you already appreciate? Do you appreciate them right away?

Director: I think you have to be careful here.

Handsome: Why?

Director: Because you'll be tempted to think in types.

Handsome: You mean you might take the new people you meet to be the same as the ones you already know even though they're not?

Director: Yes.

Handsome: A good point. And I think it especially holds when dealing with Ones.

Director: Why especially so, Handsome?

Handsome: Because every One, every true One — is unique.

160. DEGREES OF UNIQUE?

Director: What makes true Ones unique?

Handsome: Their love.

Director: Your lover is unique in her love for you?

Handsome: Yes. And I'm unique in my love for her. Do you agree?

Director: If it's truly your One? Yes, I agree. But do you think there's anything else that can make you unique?

Handsome: Well, we talked about a mind of your own. Having one makes you unique even if you've yet to find your One.

Director: So, love and a mind of your own. Is that all that makes people unique?

Handsome: I think we should also include the true love of family and friends.

Director: So any true love makes you unique.

Handsome: Yes.

Director: And is there anything else?

Handsome: No, that's it.

Director: Okay. But are there degrees of uniqueness possible? Or is it all or nothing?

Handsome: You're unique or you're not. Talking about degrees of unique is like talking about degrees of being alive or dead.

Director: I know what you mean. But when it comes to living, to being unique, would you agree there are two ways?

Handsome: What two?

Director: Always having been unique and not always having been unique.

Handsome: Those are the two ways. Always being and coming to be.

Director: Is there anything wrong with coming to be unique? Do you know what I'm asking?

Handsome: You're asking if someone who came to be unique should feel inferior to someone who was always unique.

Director: Well?

Handsome: No, that person shouldn't feel inferior.

Director: Why?

Handsome: Because who can say how hard it was to become unique? Maybe it was harder than it was for someone who was always unique to go on being unique. And if it was harder it's more praiseworthy. Do you know what I mean?

Director: I know exactly what you mean. And I think you're right.

Handsome: Good. Now let's call the server and get the check. It's gotten late and we're the last ones here. No, no. Put your money away. It's my turn to pay.

161. END

Director: So it's time to draw our dialogue to a close.

Handsome: How shall we end?

Director: With one last question.

Handsome: What question?

Director: This. If you know you're unique, would you ever be with someone who's not your One?

Handsome: Are you asking if the unique make mistakes? Of course they do.

Director: But if you're certain you made a mistake, what do you do?

Handsome: You correct it.

Director: And once you have, what comfort do you have?

Handsome: You have the comfort of the others you love.

Director: And these others, do they love us for being unique?

Handsome: Of course. And we love them for being unique. It's reciprocal that way.

Director: So we support each other in our uniqueness?

Handsome: I'd even say we enhance each other's uniqueness.

Director: How do we do that?

Handsome: By encouraging each other to have minds of our own.

Director: And what happens if love finally comes?

Handsome: What do you mean?

Director: Does our romantic love crowd these other loves out?

Handsome: No, Director. Romantic love creates an atmosphere which magnifies our love, all of our love. And that's the full life. A mind of your own, your love, and all the others you love. Don't you agree? I know you agree. Because you have a mind of your own and the love of others. And now you're going on the hunt with me — to find your One!

Director: Well, I think we should end things there. But here's one last question, one that doesn't belong to our dialogue proper.

Handsome: Yes?

Director: While we're on the hunt... will you write?

Handsome: Write?

Director: Handsome, have you really forgotten what you said at the outset? You said you might go back and write another play about love!

Handsome: But I have more important things to do now!

Director: More important than telling the truth about love?

Handsome: Let me find my true love first, my friend — and then I'll tell everyone all about it.

Printed in the United States
By Bookmasters